Northumberland Festival of the Arts

OUR PANDEMIC TIMES

A Journal in Times of Pandemic and Lockdown

Edited by
Felicity Sidnell Reid & Kim Aubrey

blue denim press

Published by Blue Denim Press Inc.
Cover design: Shane Joseph
Published in Canada
ISBN 978-1-927882-61-0

Library and Archives Canada Cataloguing in Publication

Title: Our pandemic times : a journal in times of pandemic and lockdown / edited by Felicity
  Sidnell Reid, Kim Aubrey.
Names: Sidnell Reid, Felicity, 1936- editor. | Aubrey, Kim, 1960- editor.
Description: Poems, prose, and essays.
Identifiers: Canadiana (print) 20210219726 | Canadiana (ebook) 20210219963 | ISBN 9781927882610
  (softcover) | ISBN 9781927882627 (Kindle) | ISBN 9781927882634 (EPUB)
Subjects: LCSH: COVID-19 Pandemic, 2020-—Literary collections. | LCSH: Canadian literature—21st
  century. | LCSH: Authors, Canadian—Ontario—Northumberland. | CSH: Canadian literature (English)—
  21st century | CSH: Authors, Canadian (English)—Ontario—Northumberland
Classification: LCC PS8237.C69 O97 2021 | DDC C810.8/03561—dc23

Table of Contents

Our Pandemic Times

Eight weeks after the WHO declared the Coronavirus outbreak a pandemic and countries started to take unprecedented measures to protect their citizens and prevent the spread of the virus, most of us began self-isolating while some were quarantined on returning to Canada from abroad.

We looked for ways to maintain connections in our writing community. The radio show we promote, Word on the Hills, moved its production to Zoom. The writers' group to which we belong also started to meet online. Over the months since March 2020, more and more of our contacts became virtual ones.

We have grown accustomed to a changed world. Will this experience influence how we live in the future? Isolation has affected different people differently. Some of us took to baking and making bread, others developed a passion for cleaning and clearing out cupboards and drawers, and many of us put on gardening gloves, mowed the grass and tidied up the bit of the world we could control. Some dug deep into gardening, and what wonderful gardens they turned out to be! Was it the drop in pollution levels, the good weather or the freedom of working outside, felt by those who planted seeds and celebrated their growth that produced such flourishing harvests? All these activities, as well as many others, like the great increase in people biking, walking and taking part in other healthful opportunities, can be seen as some of the positive effects of living in a time of pandemic and lockdown.

Most of us too have been able to write! This is reflected in the variety of items writers have shared on the blog, *A Journal in Times of Pandemic and Lockdown*. Some have also been busily editing older work and making it shiny and new. The Journal has provided a platform for those who wanted to share reflections, experiences and some of their recent work. As 2021 gets underway and vaccinations become available, we hope that Covid may be contained.

The editors of the Journal are pleased to be putting together this e-book as a chronicle of a year of challenges and change. However, in this time of societal distress, we shouldn't forget that universal life events continue to affect us, whether birth or death, illness or recovery, financial difficulties or a stimulus to invent new ways of doing or making things. We will feel joy or sorrow and mourn or celebrate in continuing stressful circumstances. All this will play a part in what we write or don't write. We hope that this collection will reflect the many ways in which individuals have responded to these challenges.

Felicity Sidnell Reid and Kim Aubrey, Editors

NFOTA celebrates the creative spirit of Northumberland. We believe art should be accessible to all, creativity is unlimited and collaboration makes a community strong.

SPRING 2020

The Big Apple Photo—Ted Amsden Photography
©2021

A Day in Our Pandemic Life
Shane Joseph

How does a typical day in Covidius Times flow by? Let's see, I wake up late, around 7:30 AM, and play with Facebook. Amuse myself with jokes and insults, while inhaling voluminous doses of cyber gloom. Finally, I rise around 9 AM when my body is stiffening from exercise limited to thumb movements. Breakfast is the old oatmeal and almond milk routine, spiced with raisins, wild blueberries, and cinnamon—the anti-cholesterol concoction that I can now make in my sleep.

Then it's to the newspaper for a nostalgic view of historical photos of sports when they once existed. There are more opinions in the paper nowadays, as science learns on the fly and changes its mind daily. I switch back to my smartphone—there's more interesting stuff here: Twitter, YouTube, Goodreads, e-mail, and all the non-fake-news, like CNN, CBC, BBC etc. (Is CNN fake yet?)

I go into my writing studio in my pyjamas. Nothing imaginative emerges. Last year, despite publishing four books for my publishing company, launching one of my own, running a busy travel agency, taking four extensive trips abroad, playing a lot of golf, and recovering from a cardiac arrest, I wrote two complete novels. This year, with all the time on my hands, I have written one measly short story. Is Covid-19 a disease of the mind? Does it cripple with paranoia while enveloping our headspace in an ennui that says, "Ah, well, I can always get it done tomorrow?"

Soon it's lunch—soup, bread, and a dessert treat of two squares of dark chocolate. Then back to the computer, trying to write a review of a book I took two weeks to finish. At 4 PM I wrap tools, book review unfinished, shower, change, and head out on my walk. This is the highlight of my day. I walk fast, down to the water and along the two beaches our town is blessed with. The occasional pedestrian hurriedly crosses the street upon seeing me barrelling down as if I were His

Excellency Covid himself. I stop to take pictures of the serene townscape and lake to post later on Facebook and one-up my friends who live in crowded cities or curfewed locales. I **must** capture some beauty during these Covidius Times.

Returning, I do my stretches, an important activity as my muscles atrophy from stasis and statins. Then it's time to cook—another highlight. I'm a daring cook these days. A pinch of this, a touch of that; notch up on this, tone down on that, when in doubt use everything on the spice rack. Oh, and a double shot of Irish whiskey goes well while cooking. And don't forget to top up regularly.

By the time my wife comes home (she is an essential worker, I am considered non-essential), dinner is ready, and I am in fine fettle. After a sumptuous repast, I start getting drowsy. Time to crank up Netflix, but the download fails again on an internet connection stretched to the limit in our neighbourhood full of self-isolationists.

So, I turn to the e-book purchased off Amazon, one I have been trying to get into for the last four days. Midway, everything goes quiet. Suddenly—crash! I jolt awake. I have fallen asleep reading in my comfortable chair, and my tablet is prone on the floor—mercifully, it is not broken. "I think it's time for bed," my wife says knowingly. I hastily concur.

Tomorrow will be another day, much like this one.

At This Time
Reva Nelson

I know that
Some of you have
Cleaned the stove, tidied your closets, painted your
bathroom, emptied your cupboards
Washed the floors, cleansed your cushions, vacuumed your
cars
Written three novels, painted five pictures
And accomplished countless other achievements.

I have
Talked on the phone
Watched Netflix
Read ten novels
And have been in shock.
This author of Bounce Back: Creating Resilience from
Adversity
Has not felt resilient, has not felt new energy, has not felt
creative.

However
I do rejoice
That Nature said, "Enough"
Too many pollutants, too many emissions
Too much waste

And has started to stitch up the ozone layer
Put fish back in the waters
Allowed bees to flourish
And has set us straight

In spite of ourselves.

The Upside
Cynthia Reyes

Last night, we had supper at the table for the first time in weeks. First, we prayed for all who are at risk of the virus, then we gave thanks for our blessings.

The upside of being restricted at home with family is that someone always senses when we need an uplift. Out comes a sandwich, a bowl of guacamole, or a whole meal with vegetarian meatballs, which I know is an oxymoron, somewhat like chicken balls.

We all know chickens do *not* have balls.

This morning, we cut slices of warm bread—ingredients (flour, yeast, water and salt) mixed by daughter, left to rise overnight, then, this morning, separated into loaf pans and baked.

The yummiest thing: fresh warm bread.

My daughter held her baby and we sang along with "Lovin' You" by Minnie Riperton. Minnie and husband Richard Rudolph created the song "as a distraction" for their baby daughter Maya.

My granddaughter loves to dance. Yes, at 5 months old. All you have to do is sing and move your body while holding her, and the arms and legs start to dance, while her face fills with joy and laughter.

Daughter and I got a bit emotional as we sang along:

"Stay with me while we grow old

And we will live each day in springtime"

We knew that Minnie died at age 31 when Maya (actor Maya Rudolph of *Saturday Night Live*, *Bridesmaid* and *The Good Place*) was not quite 7 years old.

Our singing faltered at the memory, but we kept going, uplifted by granddaughter's smiles and dancing.

"Want to go for a walk, Mum?" Daughter asked.

So we did, and passed three men working in front-yards.

"Gentlemen, I've found a dime!" one hollered.

"That's my dime!" another yelled from across the street.

"I was counting on that dime for my retirement!" shouted the third.

We laughed with them and continued walking.

Back home, granddaughter asleep, my husband put some cushions on the outdoor chairs. Daughter and I sat outside in "the South of France"—the name we've given our back garden since it's unlikely we'll visit the south of France any time soon.

Then, out of the blue, she asked, "Mum, how do you know what's a flower and what's a weed?"

We toured the garden beds. I pointed at the mint-like leaves of red bee-balm, describing the blooms to come, the dark-green-brown cylindrical beginnings of Ontario's flower, the trillium.

And my favourite early-spring bloomer, the blue scilla.

...then the pesky dandelions, growing between brick pavers.

"When I was younger, I thought you were weird," daughter said later. "But it was cool! I learned a lot just now—what's a bee balm, a tulip, a daffodil, a scilla and an alien."

"An alien?" her dad asked.

"An allium," she corrected herself as we all roared.

Older daughter has a small garden, and I love when she seeks my gardening advice. Then today, younger daughter, who, along with her husband, will likely buy their first house soon, took an interest in the garden.

Would it have happened if we weren't under stay-at-home orders? Maybe later, not now.

Special moments like these are the upside of a scary time. I need to mark them, and not forget them.

Blue Scilla, Photo by Cynthia Reyes

Isolation
Gwynn Scheltema

It's 2020, April 1st
I'm lying on the couch in my fourth-floor apartment
day is breaking
I've always loved the pastel washes of dawn
but things are different now

I didn't know how different mornings could be
how it was possible after living so many years
seeing so many sunrises
in so many places
and always loving that emergence—
that things could be so different now

I've always loved morning meditation
sitting silent on a spring-green mat, gratitude, breathing
in the newness and another chance at living a perfect day
finding my muse and feeling her flow of words to paper—
but words refuse to flow, it's different now

I hear voices
not from my creative well, but from silent streets
dead leaves blowing unnoticed in the empty parks
yellow tape across the vacant red-blue play slides
a lonely dog walker crossing the street to pass another
furtive dog walker masked—
the world moves differently now

I never knew stillness could feel
heavy as this winter quilt
suffocating as recirculating air in this apartment
motes of soundless stalkers settling on my hands and face
washing twice every hour to stifle them

I slept on this couch last night, in my clothes

didn't see the point of moving now that
day runs into night runs into day and
again today I will be alone
on my couch under this quilt
in my fourth-floor apartment
as day runs into night runs into day

nothing is different now

Breaking
Antony Di Nardo

the sky's been a confederate gray ever since
morning got started

fat flakes of snow streaked across the beginnings
of another April and my shoes felt tight

what I was the day before has crumbled
and hides beneath the sheets

I forage for simple shafts of light and come up empty
I find my Inbox stuffed beyond a 100 more

than I care to read   cables split the sky in two
and by the sounds of it the wind strikes me as malevolent

while peepers peeping in a videoclip I open confine me
further to a memory of days that don't count anymore

and strange thoughts of breaking free remind me
there is no music but the hum of repercussions

Photo by Ann Di Nardo

Time for Creativity
Jessica Outram

Imagine you nurtured your creativity and everything changed.

When schools closed in March the rhythm of life changed. The world shifted from out there to inside the house. Now home was the container for every aspect of our days. The boundaries between working and living blurred. What made sense now in this new way of being?

"The best way out is always through."—Robert Frost

Like many I started with the essentials. Weekly grocery trips. Daily walks in my neighbourhood. Lots of work emails and online meetings. Online shopping. More deliveries. Curbside pick-up. Long phone calls with family and friends. Creativity, something that has always been at the centre, felt like an impossibility in the midst of all the change. I gave myself permission to nap instead of create. Sometimes we get lost.

One day I signed up for an online meditation class. I started a daily meditation practice. On walks, I listened to audiobooks and podcasts about mindfulness and creating a life of intention. I learned more about energy. Creative projects found me. I started singing lessons on Zoom, worked with a new company called Theatre In Absentia (now with Northumberland Players) to direct scenes for an online version of *The Importance of Being Ernest*, and finally wrote in the mornings again.

Every week I finished a couple of paintings. Walks turned into poetic exercises in noticing metaphor. Home transformed into an expression of this rich inner self I had discovered. I painted my mailbox, planted a garden, added more light to the rooms. Soon the days were overfilled with art, poetry, and creativity spiraling through everything. What a blessing for this time to connect, to create, to find so much meaning in stillness!

We make the road by walking. Getting started can be as easy as going for a walk every day. To create is to bring something into existence. To create requires action. We begin by beginning.

Creativity is abundant. The more we use, the more we attract. If you are looking for a light out of the COVID-19 darkness, turn on your creativity. When we use creativity in one area of life it will transfer into other areas.

This year hasn't been what we predicted. We are unsure of what will happen next week and next year. With plans on hold, sadness in our communities, isolation from loved ones, losses in jobs, and news stories beyond belief, we need our inner resources to see us through. It is possible to turn this into a time of grace, love, connection, and inspiration.

"One must dare to be happy."—Gertrude Stein

Painting by Jessica Outram

Making Soup
Kathryn MacDonald

What's in the cupboard?
What's in the fridge?

She peeks here and there.
Veggies? Broth? Seasonings?

Abundance   and scarcity.

Peel.   Chop.   Substitute.
Sauté.   Simmer.   Taste.
Adjust.   Purée.

Beyond the window
sun shines   beckoning.
            Her bike's in winter storage.

Tulips
Yellow daffodils
Narcissus surely bloom
Robins and worms
Bunnies under spring Hosta leaves
A solitary swan on the river

            But an ingredient's lacking?

            Quixotic desires?
            Think Midas.

            Don your cowboy bandana.

            Substitute two feet for two wheels.

Make soup.

Great British Baking Show Haikus
Kim Aubrey

1.

Reality too harsh?
Retreat under meringue peaks
to bake a *dacquoise*

2.

What could be more real
than sugar, egg whites, and cream
beaten, then eaten?

3.

To frost sweet pastry
amidst news of plague and grief
pipes rosettes of hope.

Whoopie Pies, Photo by Kim Aubrey

A Good Life
Michael Croucher

Covid-19 is nasty and causes great anxiety. But as the saying goes, "We need reminding as much as educating." History has continually served up frightening events, wherever and whenever we've lived. But, most weren't amplified by the hysteria of social media.

I have a 98-year-old English aunt. I phone her every morning. We've talked about this. She believes, as I do, that major catastrophes occur at least once every twenty years. They are a part of life. Eventually they end, often to be quickly forgotten.

If we look at our own time-lines, with little thought we could create a list of these events. I'm not going to bore you with my entire list, but to give you an idea, here are a few that my aunt and I remembered from my younger years: German (Doodlebug) rocket attacks during the final years of WW2, post-war rationing, actually more restrictive than the war-time version, Scarlet Fever, polio and other illnesses. Most of these issues had world-wide implications.

As for the decades since, all of us could put together similar lists, starting with the Cold War's nuclear threats, terror attacks, and wars. Then SARS and other health scares. They were all serious, all frightening to a greater or lesser degree, all preceded and occasionally followed by other horrific events. But life went on. We licked our wounds and got on with it. We found enjoyment wherever we could, accomplished what we could, mourned losses and celebrated victories.

I recall these words from a Jimmy Buffet song "…some of it's magic, some of it's tragic, but I've had a good life all the way." I think life is better when experienced like that.

Quarantine Wishes
Kathryn MacDonald

black heads bobbing   *chicka-dee-dee-dee*
among winter-shrivelled barberries

goldfinches' *ti-dee-di-di*   music
lilting like waves through air

plump mourning doves in pairs
singing their sad *ooahoo oo oo oo*

congregations of ducks   *quack*ing
a family of swans silently swimming

fish in the river
and heron along the shore

turtles floating on logs
even a snake or two

children on bicycles
parents jogging along

seniors slowly strolling
young lovers embracing

our hearts want spring
and ordinary things

parks and trails
rivers and bays
the earth renewed
with grass and flowers

blue sky
corona-free

Time to Face the Virus
Carolyn Muir Helfenstein

In our innocence of what was to take place the next day, March 5, 2020, Harry and I had one last wish for our Nova Scotia holiday. We would hunt down Edgehill School for Girls, which my mother attended in 1917. Then, with family home from school and jobs, we would have one last fun supper together.

My mother, born on one of the final days of 1899 was a Newfoundlander and a storyteller. She often recalled the day she and her fellow Edgehill school friend heard the horrendous sound from a munition ship exploding in faraway Halifax Harbour on December 6, 1917, killing 2,000 people in the city and injuring over 9,000. An event she never forgot.

Harry and I found the school with ease, driving down a long driveway that must have seen horse and buggy days, and that led to a quadrangle of well-aged red brick buildings now called King's-Edgehill School. I boldly entered what appeared to be the right office and was greeted by Juanita Giles, the Database Manager, an extremely kind woman, who said, with a twinkle in her eye when she found out I was looking for an Edgehill girl, "What year? Her name again? I'll be right back."

Up the stairs she went. She came back down the staircase with the yearbook for 1917. She had copied a very important page, and there it was, "Jean Crawford, father, Henry Crawford, St. John's Newfoundland, 1917."

She also presented me with several keepsakes from the school. She wanted to know about my mother, what career did she follow when returning to Newfoundland. There was much I could have told her, but I knew my mom would be nudging me to mention that her brother, Ned Crawford, was a Rhodes Scholar who attended Oxford University, England, and later worked as a lawyer in Winnipeg. Ms.

Giles smiled broadly, "That must have been a nice item to place with his curriculum vitae."

Harry and I left with large grins creasing our aging faces, imagining what it must have been like the day young Jean Crawford approached this school as a seventeen-year-old, far from her family and her home in St. John's. Our party that evening was great fun.

On our flight back to Toronto, I thought of my visit to Memorial University Folklore Department the year before. I was surprised when they told me, "Carol, your book *Rock Solid* is about Newfoundland. You are a Newfoundlander! We want to put both your published books in our archives."

Not a Rhodes Scholarship for sure, but I think my mother would have been very pleased. Just memories now, and then time to face the virus.

Newfoundland Coast, Photo by Carolyn Helfenstein

Wearing Masks
Donna Wootton

All Sew Divas are now located on the shore of Rice Lake. They used to be in Port Hope. I needed a minor job done before my big move. Would I make the drive just for two seams? It occurred to me when I came across some material in the closet that the pink pattern would make pretty masks. I asked about the sewing jobs and yes, they were making masks, charging $2.50 each, which they donated to charity. From the leftover cloth I got ten masks. One hangs permanently on my car mirror. Three I gave away. Six fit nicely on the hooks set in the door of the hall closet in my new condo. Now they are part of my wardrobe.

When first asked to wear facial covering in public, I tried a bandana. I have a big stash of bandanas and chose one shaped perfectly with printed ducks on green cloth. I found wearing it inefficient. It kept falling down, wouldn't stay up covering my nose which was the whole point. So I abandoned my drawer full of bandanas for surgical masks. They had them for sale at the pharmacy where I picked up a prescription of only 30 pills, rationed in case the health system ran out of drugs. No point even thinking about the impact on me and others of that possible shortage. The surgical masks were expensive. I put one on to go to the bank to protect the teller from my possible contamination. Then I threw it away. I did that a few times and concluded such practices could break the bank. So I was grateful to pay for my own cloth masks.

I find wearing a mask makes my eyeglasses fog up and leaves me sweaty. As soon as I reach my car after doing errands, I pull it off. How long will we have to wear them? Into the foreseeable future we're told. The new normal. What's normal about wearing a mask? I grew up in a culture where wearing a mask meant you were a bandit. They were part of the costume for playtime. The bandit I liked best was Zorro. He was a hero, like the three musketeers. Are we heroes for wearing them now? Maybe.

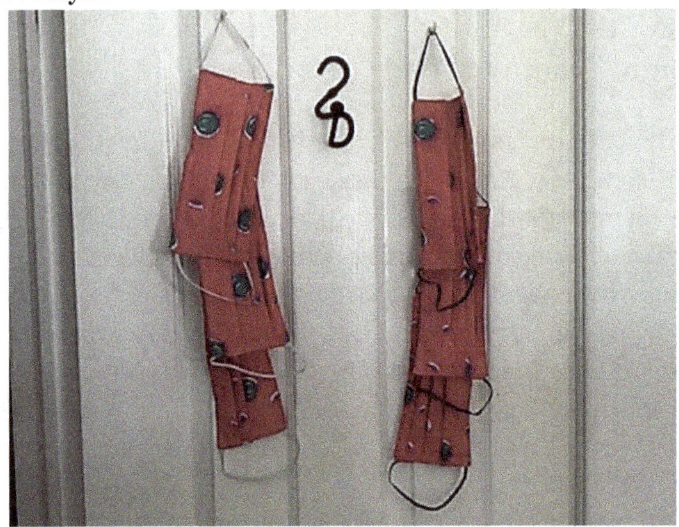

Masks, Photo by Donna Wootton

Reflections on Social Distancing
Eric E. Wright

Life has been upended by an invisible virus. The byword has become *distance*—social distance.

Mothers' Day meant distance from our kids. At least we sat on our porch six feet away from our daughter and her husband. We parted with virtual hugs. No touch. No visit from our son in Mississauga. Fortunately, he and our son in Atlanta called Mary Helen.

Since our daughter lives in a nearby village, she has taken it upon herself to get a lot of our groceries. But no hugs. No touch. As a rather stolid man, I didn't realize how much I missed the hugs of our kids and grandkids.

Then there's distance from our doctors. Appointments and blood tests cancelled. Yeah! Celebration…but wait, should we be concerned about all the regular medical decisions postponed? At least Mary Helen has been able to schedule a clinic visit and phone consultations using photos sent to her skin specialist.

Coffee with friends also meant distance. Two friends came over with lawn chairs they put up below our porch for a chinwag. All went well until a cold wind sprang up. We found them blankets so they could join us on the porch at a distance.

In April a dear friend died from Covid-19. He died isolated in the hospital. Isolated from family and friends. Dave was one of those quiet, dependable saints who demonstrate the reality of our faith. Always there to welcome new and old to the service. Tall and thin but with a grip like iron. Always available if one needed help. Always offering a cheerful countenance and an encouraging word. Not a preacher nor a teacher but a wise deacon. One of the first ones to volunteer to join a repair crew sent down south to help in the cleanup from one of their hurricanes. The first one to join the team tasked with helping to build a new church or put on a new roof for someone in straightened circumstances.

True, he was of a good age. True, he is now rejoicing, pain-free in the presence of his Saviour. But there was no gathering of relatives and friends to rejoice in his send-off and grieve his loss. Instead there was a very abbreviated grave-side burial with no more than ten attending and lasting no more than 15 minutes. Some of us looked on via zoom. How sad to view this brief acknowledgement of a wonderful man. Distant.

All the rituals attending the death of a friend or relative that have been honed over millennia to bring some closure and celebration to the passing of a life well-lived—all those have been upended. And just this week the father of a friend has died in a distant US state while she is stuck here on this side of the border. Distant.

In spite of all that is hurtful about this pandemic, some good has come of it. The technology that provides social networking has been a boon. We can zoom with our families or social groups! We can attend church remotely with a cup of coffee nearby. Well that's not so great. But here in our condo community I've noticed a happy increase in friendliness and socializing—at a distance of six feet. And of course, for the people of faith, it is a great time to rest on all those promises of Scripture. But God speed the return of touch and hugs!

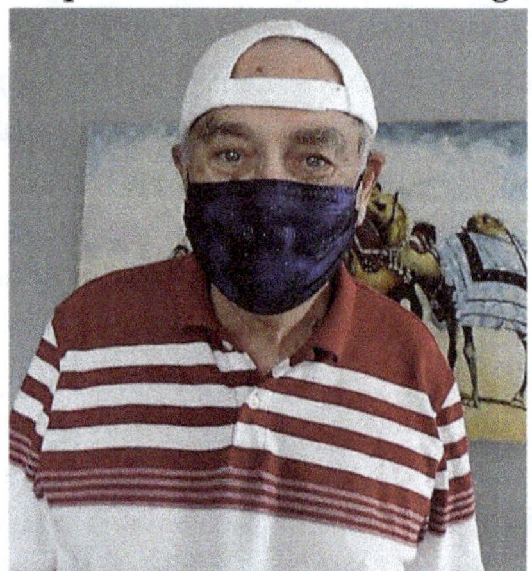

Eric Wright wearing mask, Photo by Eric E. Wright

Gwynn's Mom

A Good Death
Gwynn Scheltema

My sister contacted me by text from Zimbabwe a few days ago to tell me that my mother's step sister had died. My mind immediately defaulted to "From Covid?" After all, Carole was in her eighties, and I'm not in contact with her so had no idea if she was in a retirement home or not, and well...retirement homes these days...awful to say, but the first thought is....

Turns out, she died peacefully and not alone. She'd been living for some years with her daughter in the US and was not ill. I'm sad that she's gone, but in these strange times, at least she had good death. A good death. Wow. Would I have thought that a year ago?

I'm so sorry

My mother lives in Zimbabwe too. She lives alone in our home town Bulawayo, a 6-hour trip from my sister in Harare—and, of course, the other side of the world from me. Living alone in a decimated and violent country is her choice. Heaven knows we've offered more times than I can remember to have her come and live with either my sister or me – but that's another story.

She has a smart phone, but intermittent internet and electricity only a few hours a day, so video calls—or phone calls of any kind—are not possible. A simple text message is the only contact method we have. Add to that my mother's frustration with "using these new-fangled devices that don't work half the time and erase my typing at a drop of a bloody hat."

Nonetheless, I texted her to say how sorry I was about Carole. Such an inadequate medium. I was more concerned about my mother's loss and sadness than the fact that Carole was gone. But there was no voice inflection to impart that. The words, "I'm so sorry," seemed so empty. And "sending love and cyber hugs" so so inadequate.

Waiting for a reply

I waited for a reply. I imagined her in her house, the sun blanketing the garden in warmth outside her window. If she was checking messages, she'd be in her favourite chair, shabby now from years of use and being shared with a long succession of dogs. The tea tray would be on the table beside her, the silver leaf strainer still laid beside the milk jug even though she uses tea bags these days. Throughout the decline of Zimbabwe over the last forty years, she has insisted on maintaining the same rituals she's always known, especially those involving tea. And I knew she'd insist on maintaining a "stiff upper lip" too when she read the news.

I wasn't wrong. The reply came the next day: Thanks for your wishes. We had a special bond. I wrote an obituary and asked Steph (my sister) to post it on Facebook.

Silent heartbreak

I wanted to scream. Shout out as loud as I could that she might hear me across a whole ocean: "Yes, but how are you FEELING?"

Just as I imagined her getting the message, I imagined her reaction: "Oh," she would have said out loud to no-one. "Oh dear. How sad." And that would be an end to it. She'd reach for a tissue and wipe a tear away from the corner of her eye. She'd take a deep breath and stare out at the garden.

I have no way of knowing what she thought. Would she think on old times with Carole when they were kids? Would she think of the future? Would she think of Carole and her passing or think about anything but? I'll never know. Even if I asked her, she wouldn't say.

A good death

She is the last one of that generation now. She did what was expected of her: wrote an obituary. When it's her time to go, there will be no-one left who remembers her as a child or a young woman to write her an obituary.

And more than that—in this crazy world we live in now, I not only fear she might die a violent death or an impoverished death because of where she chooses to live. Now I also wonder if she might have to die a lonely, horrific Covid death.

I cannot change what her future will be. All I can do is wish her a good death.

Wendy 80th birthday, Photo by Stephanie Welsh

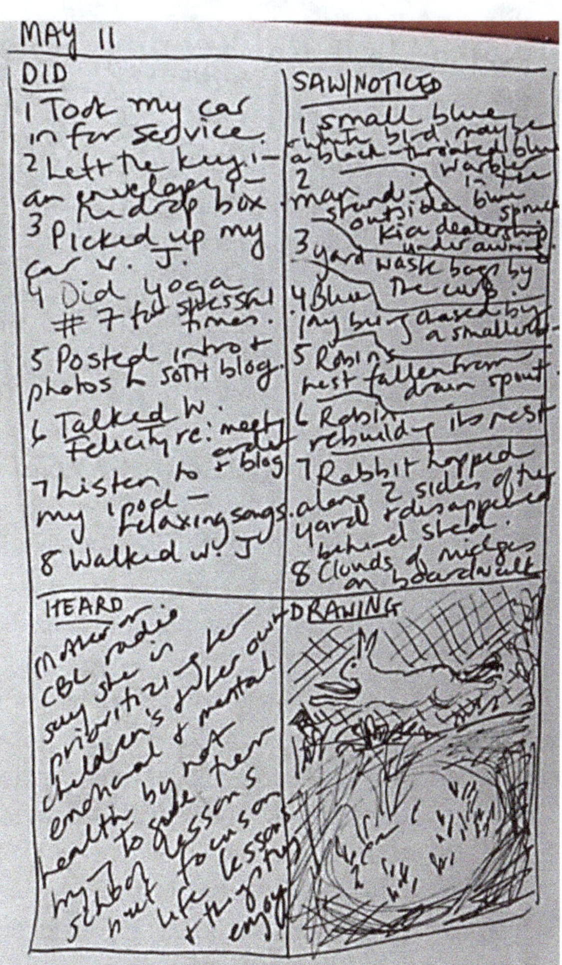

Kim's Journal, May 11, 2020

Keeping in Touch and Keeping Track
Kim Aubrey

The call for lockdown came just as my husband and I were preparing to drive to New Hampshire to care for my mother during her recovery from surgery. Her hip replacement was scheduled for March 18. On March 14 I read the Prime Minister's online message advising Canadians to stay home, and my husband read that our health insurance would probably not cover us if we went to the US.

The next day I talked to my younger brother M. in Texas. He prepared to step in and take care of Mom.

"We can't come," I told my mother. "Maybe you should postpone your surgery."

"Not going to happen," she said, determined to go ahead with the hip replacement which would relieve her pain.

But on March 16 the surgeon's office called her to reschedule for May.

My other brother E. survived a terrible traffic accident when he was nineteen. Since then he's lived with a brain injury. He and Mom share a house and are company for one another, but over the past few years, he's had trouble keeping his balance and has suffered a few bad falls. On March 19 he fell for the second time in the space of a week. Mom called an ambulance, which took him to the Emergency Room. Luckily, he didn't break any bones, but he was in pain for a month. I wanted to be there to help my mother and brother, but all I could do was call by phone and Skype, remind him to ice his shoulder, remind her to take the anti-inflammatory pills the surgeon had prescribed.

As May approached I waited for the surgeon to postpone again, but it didn't happen. My brother M. once again agreed to stay with Mom during and after her surgery. Despite my worries, the surgery was a success, no one got sick, and Mom has had a good recovery.

Since mid-March I've been talking to her and E. every day. I used to call once or twice a week, but knowing I can't visit anytime soon and aware of the danger the virus poses, I feel the need to check in more often. It's become part of my pandemic routine, like working on my novel, online yoga and Nia classes, and the journal I've been keeping since December, inspired by an exercise in Lynda Barry's wondrous book *Syllabus: Notes from an Accidental Professor*.

Barry's book is based on the writing/drawing classes she taught at the University of Wisconsin. I'm a fan of her comics and have been wanting to write/draw a graphic novel for many years now. To prepare myself, I started doing a couple of the exercises Barry set her students—a quick daily self-portrait and daily lists of seven things done, seven things seen, and one thing heard, along with another quick drawing.

I'm grateful I began this practice before the lockdown as it's been an easy and satisfying way to keep track of these pandemic days.

Kim's Journal, May 26

Cross Creek Revisited
Peggy Dymond Leavey

This pandemic makes armchair travellers of us all. Here is an entry from my journal, dated April 22, 2010:

Three people, their backs to us as we pull in, sit silently fishing from the end of a plank dock. Parked vehicles and empty boat trailers attest to other fishers somewhere out of sight.

We have come to visit the Cross Creek, Florida, home of American author Marjorie Kinnan Rawlings (1896–1953), best known for her 1938 Pulitzer Prize-winning novel, *The Yearling*. An Historic State Park since 2007, it had not been easy to find, hidden away at the side of a narrow road overhung with trees. Just as we were thinking we should turn around, we came upon the entrance.

Although we have arrived on a day when the house itself is closed to the public, the grounds are open and the affable guide welcomes us, explaining what we can still expect to see. He encourages us to stroll the many pathways and to peek in the windows of the big, Cracker-style house. I am charmed to see Rawlings' typewriter on the table in her screened-in porch.

The man leaves us then to explore on our own. It seems, however, that every time we have a question, he appears out of nowhere, crossing our path to feed rose petals to the fluffy ducklings or to rake out the chicken coops.

The heart of the Rawlings farm was once the citrus grove, and there still remain a few orange trees. Besides the house with its iron hand pump by the back door, there is also a barn, a kitchen garden, a tenant house, and a yellow 1940 Oldsmobile parked in the breezeway. Beyond the farm, vegetation grows jungle-like, cabbage palms and lush trees draped in Spanish moss. The Florida heat presses down on us. It is very still. It is as if the years have rolled back, and time has stopped here at 1940.

Cross Creek State Historical Site, photo from Wikicommons

Travel Now
Donna Wootton

Travel, during the pandemic, is on hold, especially for those of us in the high-risk category. In recent years I have traveled extensively. The last two blogs I posted were on travel. I had a shorter version of the first travel blog published in WRITE, the Writers' Union of Canada's magazine. It came out in the winter, on Family Day, the day I returned from Guatemala, where some of us took a side trip to Tikal. I wrote about that adventure in my second travel blog.

As soon as I landed, I came back to Port Hope to an offer on my house. All very dramatic, but the irony is I got published thinking I can swing it into more published pieces, only to have travel stopped.

Reluctantly I cancelled my trip to Britain scheduled for August 1. My original plan was to fly to Gatwick, on a Dreamliner no less. If you haven't flown on one you may never get the opportunity now which is a pity because the interiors of these well-designed planes have better air quality and less atmospheric pressure, so flyers don't experience jet lag as badly as on regular planes. From Gatwick airport I was planning to go to Chichester to attend a special dance workshop. Cancelled. Then I was to take the train to Bristol to pick up my granddaughter and return via train to enjoy a week-long trip on the Isle of Wight. Cancelled.

I started scheming. What if I came as planned, went into quarantine for two weeks (maybe at my friend's house in Kintbury outside Cambridge), and then traveled to Bristol to see my family.

"Consider," my son replied. What I had to consider was the impossibility of said scheme. My daughter-in-law is a frontline worker, a head nurse redeployed to ICU. I would be at risk. I am not the only grandparent in the world missing distant grandchildren. I am bitter and resentful. How long will this separation last?

And yet, I was allowed to move during the COVID-19 pandemic. (That's another story.) I am in a spacious condo with a view of the lake from a large balcony that faces north west. I see spectacular sunsets. I have wonderful neighbours. We make and share meals. I am able to get out for social distancing walks.

I knew the previous owners of this condo and recognized it as a special place. They were long-time supporters of Horizons, the NGO I travelled with to Panama, Costa Rica, and then Guatemala. After more than a dozen years volunteering with them, fundraising for their partners in Central America, I finally got to enjoy meaningful travel to some of the places I had helped support.

Now my fear is I will not be able to travel in the future even if I'm healthy and willing and able. Will the world open up again?

Donna in Guatemala, Photo by Ulrike Bender

Baracoa's malecon leads to a long, long beach and, eventually, a fishing village. Photo by Kathryn MacDonald

The Doves Seem to Croon Tippy Canoe Tippy Canoe
Kathryn MacDonald

--Baracoa and Boca de la Miel, Cuba

1

Rain falls overnight
cleansing heat and dust of day
susurrus song on the pillow.

Travelling news greets morning
    airlines suspending flights
    a case of coronavirus at home
    factories and daycares closed
    the mantra of self-isolation repeated
                        and repeated
while the sun rises above Baracoa
                    island town
of ocean waves and mountain breezes.

You feel a bit like Robinson Crusoe.

2

Woodcut visions of medieval plague
    bodies stacked and dangling from carts
    emaciated people leaning from balconies
cross your mind before you quickly wipe
them aside.

3

Walk miles of ocean shore
to lounge upon a sheltered beach.
Eat *uva caleta*   grapelike berries
from the tree of Columbus' cross.
Crack almond shells with a stone.

At the small fishing village of Boca de la Miel
listen to riffs of Spanish voices
drift across Made's verandah
    devour fried *platano*
    sip ice-cold *cerveza*
walk home to your *casa* on Calle Maceo
close to the *malecón*.

4

From your small balcony   roof-top high
you listen to doves cooing in their dovecot
tippy canoe   tippy canoe
a rooster crowing.
                You wonder
if you've slipped into Alice's rabbit hole.

Night's rain has emptied clouds.
The sullen sky has changed to blue.

Time flattens like a Dali watch.
The doves sing their haunting song.

Boca de la Miel, Cuba. Photo by Kathryn MacDonald

Fishing, Photo by Felicity Sidnell Reid

Wanderings of the Mind
Felicity Sidnell Reid

Recently I came across part of a novel I started writing a number of years ago, then put away and more or less forgot. Since re-reading it I've been trying to continue the story, which has allowed me to "travel" in this time of Covid, since the novel is set in northeast Thailand near the Cambodian and Vietnamese borders.

I pulled out books of faded photographs, guide books, one of Thai phrases and even a journal and settled down to recall the excitements and challenges I experienced travelling alone to an unknown place, where I didn't know the language and where I had committed to teaching English at a teachers' college for six months...

Thais are a wonderfully hospitable people. I was assigned a house on the campus and frequently taken to town to shop and eat out, and on explorations of the countryside, as well as to parties, weddings, special events like the Elephant Festival in Surin, and to teachers' conferences in Bangkok and Chiang Mai, where my colleagues made sure I saw all the sights.

Every morning I woke about five to a delicate pink dawn and the harsh but cheerful sound of local roosters crowing. It was the coolest part of the day. Often a little breeze would be shaking the papaya and tamarind trees in my yard. It was a pleasure to stand behind the shutters of my bedroom listening for the musical clinking which preceded the appearance of orange-robed young monks, tapping on the bowls they carried. Marching along the road, they were met by my neighbours who knelt at the sides of the street to "make merit," *tak bat*, by offering up food taken back to the temple to be shared with the monks' elders. The smell of the dust kicked up by their bare feet mixed with that of the food created a unique odour, both dry and spicy.

Food came in every sort of variation from a basic *pad thai* of rice, vegetables and fish sauce, or morning glory stir-fry at the night market, to elaborate banquets where vegetables and fruit were sculpted into flowers and every dish was a piece of art. When I was invited to visit the nearby town, we commonly ate at the duck and sticky rice bar, sitting on high stools, the sides of the bar open to let in the breeze.

Students liked to picnic in the park around the town's reservoir. Sitting on the dry spiky grass under flame trees in scarlet blossom, they played stringed and wind instruments. At parties everyone took turns singing. Some, trained as classical dancers, performed at college events.

In the villages, rice was still cut with scythes, the harvesters moving across the fields like dancers, the water buffalo allowed to wander, sometimes into my garden, and intricately patterned silks and cottons woven on hand looms. In the town, the well-off and educated had every possible mod con and technical device to hand, and transport ran the gamut from overloaded bicycles, often carrying whole families, to chauffeured limousines.

Wonderful memory! Once stimulated, I am back in that place where plumbago and bougainvillea pour over walls and lotus float on a pond as I walk to my morning class.

Thai Cattle, Photo by Felicity Sidnell Reid

Shelter
Kim Aubrey

Sand slows shoes, shapes
this walk into meditation.

Silver eyes flash from the dark inside
the swallow's house atop its slender pole.

Wind and sun perform their alchemy
on Lake Ontario, conjure

jewel tones of my homeland
Bermuda's reef-encircled seas.

On the point, a woman in a red coat
passes under a bent bough

makes the space beneath
briefly resemble a pop tent.

Mermaids dance on a pink pail tilted
from a branch, waiting to be filled.

The day tips, sways, pauses at the twig end
of Week Eight's distancing and isolation,

offers its emptiness to contain,
meet, shelter whatever comes.

Pink Poppy, Photo by Kim Aubrey

Pandemic Trilogy
Marie-Lynn Hammond

1.
Barely Noticed

spring
belatedly crept up on us
we barely noticed

we hauled up all the drawbridges
barricaded ourselves in
against the pestilence

but it invaded by stealth
and left us powerless
as peasants

and while we
counted potatoes
and washed
our hands
over
and
over
and
over
buds swelled
grass grew
squirrels nonchalantly
went about their business
birds sang unruffled
in the blossoming warmth

and in the flowerbeds
the grape hyacinths
sprang upward

in triumph
tiny tender spears
of royal hue

while we cowered
and sickened
and died

the greening earth
barely noticed

Grape Hyacinths, Photo by Marie-Lynn Hammond

2.

Everything and Nothing

I fear when this is over
that we will have learned everything
        and nothing
        that we will zoom back to "normal"

        (As if the way things were before was normal—
        humans heaping ruin on the verdant earth,
        leaving blood and tempests, extinction and empty
                                dust in our wake)

Like an old film reel rewinding
the skies over China will morph

from their new blue
to choking orange
workers will back up
return to factories
to churn out tawdry goods
none of us really need
cars and people will swarm in reverse
through our now empty cities
to be devoured and spat out
over and over
by cogs and sprockets
    ones and zeros
  the market's insatiable maw

And the golden butterfly in Brazil
newly emerged into sunlight
   and fragile survival
will be extirpated by a key stroke
in some mining czar's office
on the seventeenth floor

Our newfound kindness
as sweet and plump as a nectarine
will shrivel and shrink
to a stony
kernel

And the wild goats and deer
now grazing on suburban lawns
and lolling in the empty, sun-warmed streets
    will gallop backward
   to their old haunts
  their shrinking forests

to nothing

Caribou by Marie-Lynn Hammond

3.

The Plague

This winter drove us, hard and cruel;
We suffered its barbaric rule.
It killed our spring, gave us instead
this sickness and unending dread,
as, distantly, we mourned our dead.

But now, this first mild spell in May,
the lake lies calm and blue today.
Frost-blighted buds, though brown and curled,
persist, and soon will be unfurled
as if no change has marked our world.

Yet change has come, with surely more,
and likely worse, for us in store;
for we have desecrated all,
have fouled our nest with toxic sprawl,
and hastened Eden's second fall.

We poison land and sea and air,

and stamp out species everywhere;
we rape the earth for oil and gold
(until the centre cannot hold)
and breed like rabbits, uncontrolled.

Oh, how we breed and breed and breed!
Eight billion hungry mouths to feed.
And greed gets overlaid on top,
so some must starve while others shop.
But want trumps all; we do not stop.

And yet the lake is calm today...
it seems to hold the plague at bay.
The earth in balance once again;
no raging flames, no hurricane,
no drought or ceaseless, flooding rain.

The robins preen, spring peepers peep,
the sap still runs, the trout still leap.
But can it be forever thus?

No. Nature *should* kick up a fuss,
for now we know: the plague is us.

Blue Lake, Photo by Marie-Lynn Hammond

Fading Stars
Christopher Black

While robins woke to fading stars,
That drew fat worms to morning doom,
And tired hands sought coffee jars,
Still half in dream and nightly tomb,
While prostitutes and presidents,
Walked secret streets, or secret rooms,
And madmen claimed it all made sense,
But nightly danced in drunken fear,
While others stared in innocence,
But couldn't help a sudden tear,
Rising from their aching hearts,
For those they lost they once held dear,
A message came from foreign parts,
Of something strange passed through the air;
As if a fusillade of poisoned darts,
That pierced the old and young, the sad and fair,
In silence, swift, and thus, unseen,
As Satan climbing Heaven's stair,
His strength renewed and body lean,
To reclaim his old authority,
And sit the chair where God had been,
Sans remorse, regret, sans pity,
First one succumbed and then the many,
From east to west, in town, in city,
The working poor lost every penny,
And sat alone, apart, in wonder,
For them escape there was not any,
As the world around them broke asunder,
For existence cares not what your name,
Or what day they put you under,
And while many played the ancient game,
Of searching entrails for some secret reason,
A bleating scapegoat they could blame,
Others knew we'd had our time, our run, our season,

Had squandered all, destroyed the world,
Against Life itself had plotted treason,
So down the great abyss were hurled.

Photo by Ann Di Nardo

The Road to Gesualdo
Erika Rummel

(An excerpt from *The Road to Gesualdo*, published by D. X. Varos, Ltd. in 2020)

Carlo Gesualdo, Prince of Venosa, was a sixteenth century composer and musician. The town of Gesualdo in Campania was also the place where he lived.

Spring was in the air. The capes of the two ladies strolling in the garden were fluttering in the warm breeze. It was a glorious day, but Livia was in a dark mood.

"Something is not right," she said to her mistress. "Every time I mention Prince Carlo's name, people lower their eyes and fall silent. What are they holding back?"

"I don't want to know," Leonora d'Este said and heaved a sigh. "What's the use of chasing rumors? The contract is signed. I must do my duty and marry the man my brother has chosen for me."

Livia threw up her hands in frustration. "You must do your duty! You must do as your brother says! And what if it turns out that Prince Carlo is a monster?"

"He isn't," Leonora said. She held out a pendant dangling from a gold chain around her neck. Prince Carlo had sent her a locket with his portrait. She opened it for Livia to see. "You may judge for yourself," she said.

The man in the portrait looked young and handsome.

"He has sensitive lips, don't you think?" Leonora said.

Livia didn't agree. "They look cruel to me."

"Oh, Livia! I couldn't love and obey a man who is cruel!" Leonora said,

Livia took her mistress' arm and patted it fondly. "I didn't mean to make you uneasy," she said...

It's true, she thought. Women have no say in marriage matters. Leonora was obliged to marry a man she did not know and might not be able to love. Livia knew her admirer Pietro very well and loved him dearly but... she had no dowry, and Pietro had no money of his own. He could not afford to marry her.

Livia forced herself to stop thinking about Pietro and took up the conversation again. "What does your brother say about the Prince?"

"I had only one question: Will I be able to love Carlo Gesualdo? But Cesare doesn't care about love. Wealth and standing are all that count with him."

"Let me make inquiries," Livia said. "I'll ask Pietro. He was present at the marriage negotiations and can tell us what kind of a man Prince Carlo is."

... But Pietro was puzzled as well... He had witnessed a strange scene during a hunting party arranged for the Prince... in the forest ... where a camp had been set up.

Early in the morning Pietro was woken by the sound of a horse neighing. He parted the tent flap and saw a solitary rider leaving the camp. The Prince! Pietro thought. He sensed an adventure coming his way and followed the rider. They were going in the direction of the river. Prince Carlo stopped, dismounted, and walked slowly toward the riverbank which dropped precipitously to the water's edge some twenty feet below. Did he not realize how close he was to the brink, how close to taking a headlong fall into the river? The Prince was leaning forward now—Pietro shouted a warning and set off at a run. Without stopping to think, he tackled the Prince bodily and pulled him back. Don Carlo hung in his rescuer's arms like a puppet, stiff, silent, insensate. Pietro lowered him gently to the ground and kneeled down beside him. The Prince's face was pale, his mouth contorted and moving strangely as if he was chewing his tongue...Pietro fetched help, but the Prince's steward did not exactly thank him...

He fixed Pietro with a hard stare...

Pietro bowed. He understood that he had seen what he was not supposed to see. But...he could not make sense of the incident. Was the Prince suicidal? Was he possessed? Was he suffering from the "sacred disease"—the falling sickness?

The Road to Gesualdo

Dream Fox, Painting by Katie Hoogendam

We Bathe our Bananas: A Pandemic Fairy Tale
Katie Hoogendam

Atom knew Evie was mostly drunk now, most of the time. The kids didn't seem to notice, thanks to the enchantment of childhood. And who could blame her? The pandemic was crazy. They'd been cooped up for nearly a month—no walks, no playgrounds, no school, no work (for Evie), no trips to the cottage—no trips to the grocery store, for that matter. Only Costco deliveries, coconut oil and gluten free crackers, toilet paper if they were lucky. And then the fact that Evie's mom passed away less than a year ago, after a decade of chronic illness. So he couldn't blame Evie for being mildly buzzed pretty much all day on their stock of homemade wine. Atom wondered why they weren't having more sex—what else was there to do? *But maybe what I'm wondering is whether we are having as much sex as our friends. Why do I care about this? Do I care?* He checked his Facebook and made a mental note to order their fair-trade coffee in bulk.

Evie was embarrassed about the day drinking. For a while, in her early 30s and after the miscarriages—so many miscarriages—it was all too overwhelming and she drank a lot. *Why wouldn't I drink?* She thought at the time. *I'm grieving. Anyone would drink. Even my therapist understands.* But she hadn't told her therapist. And then she was able to have kids after all, and usually, she was just too tired to drink, or maybe actually content. In any case, she had forgotten about the power of being numb, until lately. Remembering came fast.

Mom, can I have a rice cake? There are no rice cakes. Can I have an apple, then? There are no apples. Here's a peanut butter sandwich. You guys can watch a show on my computer. Yeah!

No apples. No rice cakes. Soon, maybe no peanut butter? No bread? No flour to make bread? What the hell are we going to do? Evie poured more wine. *Just don't open a second bottle.*

Atom blasted into the kitchen from outside, cheeks flushed, body delicious with fresh air. *I think we need a project.*

Okay. Evie steeled herself for Atom's LATEST BIG IDEA. *Like what?*

Like animals, maybe? Chickens? Atom's eyes were shiny. *Or a garden? Doesn't that seem like a good idea, I mean, regardless? We could be self-sustaining. We could eat fresh eggs every day for breakfast! We could give carrots to our neighbours!*

[Toronto's police are patrolling in cars, on bikes, on horseback, en force, to make sure people are following social distancing bylaws. Tickets will be issued to those not keeping physical distance...] Evie turned the goddamn radio off.

She tried not to roll her eyes. *Yeah, I guess, chickens maybe, but I've never gardened. Are you going to be in charge of this?* Evie's mom had been a big gardener. She lived in the garden; she smelled like tomato vines. Thank God she hadn't lived to see this chaos. *Thank God I was with her then, before the borders closed.* Every day feels like a Margaret Atwood novel. Police are ticketing people for walking too close to one another. Intimacy is ominous. House parties are would-be massacres. Reality is surreal. Surreality. We wash our groceries in the sink as though they were our babies. We bathe our bananas.

Well, yeah. Atom looked deflated. *Yeah, I could be in charge of the garden. I just thought—*Evie glared at him—*I guess I thought it might be good for you. You could just—be outside with the kids all day. They could run around and you could dig and plant, and just be happy outside, you know?*

Evie plunked her glass on the counter. *Yeah, well. I'm glad you want me to be happy. I don't need you to manage me. The kids won't just "run around," you know? They require almost constant interaction from me. You can do your work on the computer all day in the basement, but I barely have three seconds to myself to go to the bathroom, much less grow and harvest a bounty of vegetables, enough to feed the neighbourhood!* Evie breathed deeply through her nose. Her therapist had suggested practicing mindfulness. Most of the time she felt a big fuck-you about mindfulness. *How could I possibly be any more present in this present moment, pressed in on all sides, trapped in the house, amputated from the outside world?*

Atom regarded her, this woman he had loved for so many years. Evie was increasingly distracted, as if her consciousness were being sliced up, severed into pieces. *What was that Egyptian story? Of the woman cut up and sent off? Isis and Osiris. No wait, that was Osiris who got cut up. The other one, in the bible maybe. The concubine? Whatever.* Atom could see that something was happening to Evie, but he felt helpless to do anything about it. She seemed to exist behind a thousand veils.

Atom moved in closer. *I'm sorry babe. I'm not trying to manage you. I just want you to be happy. To not have to*—he motioned to the wine breathing surreptitiously in a child's juice glass—*you know, all the time.*

Evie grimaced. *Geez, Atom. I probably wouldn't "you know all the time,"* she picked up the juice glass, raised it to her lips, *if the world weren't falling apart all around me. You're working more than ever, and I'm alone with the kids all day, with nowhere to go. Things are really shitty right now, you know? You know that, right? You're on planet Earth too?*

Atom pulled Evie to his chest. *You don't have to be mean. I know this is hard on you.* He smelled her hair.

Evie let out a long sigh. *I should make dinner.* Atom kissed Evie's forehead and ambled toward the living room where he leaped onto the Ikea sectional, eliciting shrieks of glee from the kids.

Organic macaroni and cheese, frozen pizza, soy milk, brown rice. *Shit.* Evie dreaded meals, felt guilty for not caring more about nurturing her family with hearty sustenance during the global pandemic, a subject currently trending among the wives and mothers of Instagram—#pandemicpasta#pandemicpolenta (*#pandemicpatriarchy?*). *Imagine your personal utopia, how would you nourish yourself?* a guided meditation once instructed her. Coffee, cigarettes, graham crackers, full stop.

The next day, Atom dug up enough earth for a small garden plot. Evie watched out the window over the kitchen sink. Atom waved, smiled. Evie let the curtain fall.

The late April air was electric, hard rains intoxicating. Evie sobbed in time with the thunder. Finally, some catharsis. The bare plot stared back at her from the kitchen window, a gaping maw of crisscrossed soil opened under torn-up sod. It reminded Evie of something. She lifted her shirt, looked down at the long scars where the caesareans had been.

Finally, the rain stopped. Spring was in full swing now, trees reaching out with buds like fists poised to open. To her knowledge, Atom had yet to procure seeds for the garden. He still claimed it would be his project. Evie decided to stay quiet. If the plot became nothing more than a barren mudpuddle, that would be fine with her.

Summer solstice and the kids screamed all day. The Prime Minister invoked a federal emergency. Over 25,000 people dead in Canada from the virus. Over one million worldwide. Borders closed to all North American trade. Costco deliveries drying up. Atom and Evie still had coffee and toilet paper, though no bananas. Atom had ordered some seeds but had planted nothing. The wine was almost gone.

That was when the weird stuff started to happen.

It was probably midnight, though clocks were really starting to lose their meaning. Atom and Evie had been up late binge-watching a Netflix miniseries about a dysfunctional Swedish stepfamily and their foibles but still, Evie couldn't find sleep. The moon must've been just about full because it filled the window with a light so brilliant she felt eerily surveilled, the panopticon of the gods shining one numinous, silver beam from their metaphysical tower on high.

Evie sat up in bed and looked out the window. If she tilted her head, she could see the plot. In the moonlight, it looked like a freshly covered grave. She scooched her body to get a better view. She blinked—a flash of movement—blinked again. *What was that?* All nerves, she got out of bed, snuck through the house to the front door where her black rubber boots lay akimbo, slipped them on and ventured outside. At the edge of the plot sat a small red fox, moonsheen casting her slick coat ethereal, a shiny beast. The vixen turned, locked eyes with Evie. It was then that Evie noticed the chicken in the fox's mouth. *A chicken! Oh God!* She ran toward the fox. Shaking her fists, Evie hissed through clenched teeth, *Drop it! Drop that! Get out of here!* The fox bounded off into the dark woods behind the house, chicken locked in her jaws.

Evie's heart sank. *The chickens!* The kids would be so upset to lose one, despite Evie and Atom's sit-down with them about predator and prey, the inevitability of death. She made her way to the coop, swung open the door. All seemed peaceful. How had the fox gotten in? The hens peered at her curiously. She counted. *One, two, three...eight.* All eight were there? Had she somehow imagined it? Maybe it wasn't a chicken in the fox's jaw after all, maybe it was a baby grouse, or some other kind of wild bird. Evie tried to knit her memories back together. She was sure it was a chicken, but she must have been mistaken. Or maybe one of their neighbours had chickens, and the fox just happened to be sauntering through their yard on the way back to her den. That must be it. Evie secured the coop door and made her way back to the house, to bed.

Chicken, Photo by Katie Hoogendam

Days passed. Schools, normally out for the summer anyway, remained shuttered indefinitely. Food banks struggled to keep up with demand. Most everyone they knew was on government assistance of some kind. Atom continued to work, though at reduced hours. The kids had become acclimated to this new pattern of staying at home, of not seeing friends, of always having both parents around. In some ways, the isolation begat a sense of wholesomeness within the family. They made their food from scratch, baked bread (a lot of bread), played board games and generally rooted in place. It appeared to Evie that Atom had forgotten entirely about planting a garden, but she wasn't about to bring it up. So far, they had been able to get by on a freezer full of frozen vegetables and the occasional, unpredictable, assortment of fruits and veggies from the grocery store. Everything was delivery-only now, to spare the workers and the general population from contact. The government had imposed strict stay-in-place measures, and no one was supposed to go further than one kilometer from home, if you were lucky enough to have a home. Several thousand across Canada were being housed temporarily in Best Westerns, Comfort Inns, school gymnasiums.

This part, this forced limitation of personal space that was starting to drive so many people batty—more than batty, really, Canada was in the throes of what looked to become a nationwide mental health crisis—was not the worst part for Evie. With the dwindling supply of alcohol on hand, and the cache offered by the liquor stores similarly endangered, Evie recognized that she had to divorce herself from the warm numb of wine. This would be difficult, to let go of one more balm, one more reminder of life past, but perhaps not as difficult as she might have expected. There was a lucidity coming over her (or maybe it was dissociation? She wouldn't know, having had to give up on her therapist weeks ago to save cash) and it had as much to do with her drying out on the booze as with the otherworldly events taking place on her property every night.

First, it was the fox, and Evie had dismissed what happened then as a trick of mind. The next night, though, it was an owl—a Great grey owl, sitting just where the fox had been, with a chicken (Evie was sure this time) in her talons. The owl itself appeared larger than she imagined an owl to be, larger than life, really, and totally unafraid of Evie. Something about her gaze felt vaguely human, and instead of chasing the owl off, Evie moved toward her cautiously. When she stopped about a metre in front of the creature, the owl adjusted the chicken in her grip and with one great swoop, took off for the trees. Evie counted the chickens again, none missing.

The next night, a coyote. Bird held loosely in her fangs, the coyote appeared to be waiting for Evie to arrive. Evie called out, as if to a stray dog. *Here girl, here girl.* She didn't know what else to do. The coyote did not move. Evie lowered herself to her haunches, made eye contact with the beast. Something changed in the air. The coyote, suddenly alert, electrified, jumped to her feet. She ran past Evie, her dusty bristle tickling Evie's arm as she pivoted for the woods, chicken and all.

Evie asked around this time, texting her neighbours, posting on their group Facebook page. No one had chickens. Nearly a month had passed since her initial encounter with the fox, and still every midnight, an animal with a chicken in her mouth and yet no chickens missing from her own flock. But it didn't end there.

After the first few weeks of midnight forays, Evie noticed a change in the garden plot. Tiny green shoots were popping up from the ground. *So Atom planted the seeds after all!* Evie was relieved. She regretted her reaction weeks before, when Atom suggested she quit drinking and start planting. At the time, she felt micromanaged and defensive. That was before grocery store shelves emptied out. Before oatmeal was hard to come by. Before "DIY Bidet" was a popular search on YouTube. Everything was moving so fast. Now the idea of growing a garden felt like the right and necessary thing to do; virtuous, even— liberation borne of desperation. *But when had he planted the seeds? And why would and how could Atom, so terrible at keeping secrets, keep his gardening a secret?* She would ask him in the morning.

I didn't plant any seeds. Atom stared at her over a precious cup of fair-trade, organic coffee. *I thought about it, but it seemed like you didn't want a garden. I couldn't handle any more conflict, so I just dropped it.* They walked out to the garden together. The plot looked as empty as it had when Atom first turned the soil. Like a fresh grave. No evidence of life. Evie was bewildered. *I swear, there was an orderly line of green plants popping up, just last night!* Atom pulled her close. *Stress does weird things, babe. It was probably just the moonlight playing tricks on your eyes.* She hadn't told him about the animals.

But it wasn't just the moonlight playing tricks on her eyes. If she hadn't felt so lucid, she would be afraid, but Evie wasn't afraid. If she was delusional, her delusions were florid. Each night, without fail, she came face to face with a beast, and each night, the green shoots grew bigger until mid-summer when the plants came into themselves— cucumbers, kale, tomatoes, carrots—even fledgling corn! Evie couldn't believe it but neither could she doubt what she saw—and felt—and smelled—and eventually tasted, the tomato's gelatinous insides clinging to her mouth and chin, her sleepy palate springing back to life. Had she ever eaten a tomato this good? And there were tomato worms too, of course. And weeds. The first few times she tended the garden she wore gloves but later cast them aside. Waking to find fresh dirt under her nails the next morning, Evie smiled, her entire body vibrating sensuously from some forgotten source deep within.

The summer lingered on. Birdsong seemed louder, cacophonous even. The President of the United States had fallen ill but was expected to recover. The death toll spiked at the beginning of August—the heat had not diminished the virus as the experts had hoped. Families were organizing reunions, normally hotdogs and beer at the Legion pavilion kind of things, over Zoom or one of the other videoconferencing apps that had popped up over the past months. Coffee, coconut oil, gluten free crackers—it was hard to believe these things had once been staples of modern existence. Hunger found new haunts. When their daughter's old preschool teacher emailed the parents to ask if they would consider donating pantry items to help some of the other families who struggled to access food, Evie had an idea.

In times like these, Evie realized (her wine was all gone now) you either had to surrender all hope or put on your big girl Spanks and holler a tremendous "FUCK YOU!" at Misfortune. She grabbed a few empty bins from the basement and made her way to the garden. She harvested everything ripe enough to pick and left the rest to grow. When she was finished, her bins were full to the brim. A cornucopia—including carrots for the neighbours—after all.

She lugged the hefty bins inside and left them in the middle of the kitchen so they would be the first things Atom and the kids would see the next morning. Evie understood this as an experiment—an experiment whose results would either confirm her total break from reality or, perhaps even more disconcerting, reality's total break from conventional narrative. Evie closed her eyes. *The flora and the fauna and the familiar unfamiliar.* She nestled into the fetal position and pulled a deep breath into her lungs. *Let it go, Evie.*

Unbelievably, she slept in. Evie raced downstairs. *Mama! Mama!* There they were, her little family, assembled in the kitchen in their pajamas. Her daughter was halfway through a cucumber and her son was taking his first bite of a dirt-encrusted carrot. Evie's body smiled. Atom was leaning against the counter. His eyes met hers; they said, *Care to explain?*

Do you share with your children things totally beyond their comprehension? Beyond your own? Do you risk their feelings of safety and security, just so they might experience the limits of their own understanding? Is wonder worth chaos? The family stood together on the plot. *Here's the dirt,* Evie grabbed a handful of soil and placed it in her children's small palms. *It looks empty now,* Evie motioned to the bare patch of ground, still unmolested by errant bluegrass. *But at night, this ground is transformed. There's a whole big garden here!* Atom eyed her warily. *Can we see it, Mama? We want to see the garden!*

Atom and Evie watched stand-up on Netflix, argued gently about comedy in the "Pandemic Era" as it was now being called. They brushed their teeth. They fumbled around in the dark with their bodies. They fell asleep. Around midnight, as she always did, Evie jerked awake. Atom shifted in his sleep. Evie considered checking things out before summoning Atom and the kids but decided against it. Whatever there was to encounter, they would encounter it together.

Atom, get up. Evie rocked his shoulder. *Atom.* He turned. They woke the kids and made their way outside.

When they reached the garden, her daughter gasped. *A coyote! It has one of our chickens!* Evie had forgotten to tell them about the beasts. *Don't worry, it's okay. Check the coop, they're all there.* They did. They were. And the garden was there, too, lush and verdant as ever.

The kids dove into the green jungle with abandon, inspecting vines for baby cucumbers. A garter snake hushed through the underbrush. The fireflies were thick. Atom pulled Evie to his side. *Oh my God, Love. This is insane. This is beautiful. I don't understand any of it.* Evie could feel Atom's heart beating like crazy beneath his ribcage. She leaned down and picked two perfect cherry tomatoes. She handed one to Atom and popped the other into her mouth.

They stood quietly for a time, watching the kids. Evie turned, grabbed Atom's hands, met his eyes. *I think it's simple, really. I think we just need to keep coming to the garden, and taking care of it, and eating from it, and giving it away. I think that's what we're supposed to do here—just keep giving it away.*

Art in Pandemic, Photo by Katie Hoogendam

SUMMER 2020

Lilies by Ann Di Nardo

Petunias in Time of Pandemic
Diane Taylor

Lockdown meant lots of time on my hands. How should I make good use of these extra hours? I looked out my south-facing window and saw the same view that I'd been seeing for the past ten Junes. The hill that sloped steeply westward now overgrown with grass that came up to my chin, two very tall black walnut trees midway down the hill with lush green canopy way up high, and a few straggly cedar trees at the bottom of the hill that were really cute against the east fence when they were little but now urgently needed trimming.

Hmm. If I were to un-straggle those cedars, what kind of new view could I create? No longer young and strong as I was when I bought this place, I tried to think of someone who might like a little yard work. No one. A few days later while driving downtown I happened to see a young man whom I'd met at a local dinner. Maybe? I sent a Facebook note. He responded with a yes!

Curly black hair tinged with gray, tall and slim, Rohan arrived with a new pair of work gloves one evening after work. A visitor! A rather rare happening in this time of pandemic. With snippers and saw we cut back about half the cedars at the east fence and all the ones on the south fence. That corner began to look spacious. We pulled dirt from the hill to level off the ground against both fences thus giving beds for...shrubs? Flowers? Vines? Birdbath? Endless possibilities! We stood back and admired the space we were creating.

We knew we should be working at a distance, six feet. But when sawing big pieces of trunk, it helped him when I stood on the other end to stabilize them. When I was walking down the four steps to the garden, as we now called the new space, sometimes he was coming up. I'd have to say we were a little too casual.

Let's talk about pay, I said.

No, no, he said, *I just want to help.*

But, I said ...

No, he said.

Well, we'd work something out.

I made a trip up to Baltimore Garden Nurseries to make my choices. Two viburnum shrubs not in bloom, a clematis not in bloom, and a yarrow not in bloom. For bloomin' colour I picked up a plant that had several bright purple flowers. I didn't even know what it was. Didn't care. Rushed it home (with the others), dug a hole, added water and composted manure, put in the plant. Now the space looked like a garden. Flowers in time of pandemic. A little revolution in the midst of this other revolution going on, the one that tells us we are all interdependent.

My sister came the next day to see my pandemic garden and said she liked my petunias.

Petunias? Where?

There, those purple flowers.

Really? They're petunias?

Yes, dear. She said in the tone of voice she uses when she thinks I'm an idiot.

Rohan came over a few more times. Then there was a message from him. He couldn't come over again for a while because he'd been in close contact at work with a co-worker who was being tested for the virus. I replied that if his co-worker was positive, he, Rohan, would need to be tested, and me too. He said he was sure we would be fine because some time had elapsed since the contact. He'd let me know on Tuesday. Today is Tuesday. Of course there is next to no chance it will be positive...on the other hand, Covid-19 is still finding bodies to inhabit...

In the meantime, the revolutionary petunias shout freedom in my backyard and bloom on in flamboyant disregard of the virus. I can almost hear the joy.

Petunias, Photo by Diane Taylor

Outdoor Activities During A Pandemic
Donna Wootton

Tai chi in the backyard overlooking Lake Ontario. What could be better than practicing on a private lawn? The invitation came when I bumped into someone from my Monday and Thursday Tai Chi classes. We both confessed we missed doing Tai Chi and weren't very disciplined about practicing on our own. There's an energy in doing Tai Chi with others. We're working on having more people join in.

Swimming in my former neighbour's backyard pool. Her pool is smack in the middle of her stunning backyard garden which has been featured in the ACO garden tour, as was mine. Watching the sun setting on the red bark of the tall pine trees in the ravine was nostalgic.

Cycling in Cobourg is very popular. Bicycle sales have gone through the roof everywhere. Here the roads and paths along the waterfront are mostly flat, so no need for too many gears. There is always an offshore breeze to cool a rider on these very hot days.

BBQ in a friend's backyard. Now that I live in a condo, I cannot barbeque so appreciate any invitation to dinner. Since I live close, I could walk home after drinking, a healthy choice. My friend got to show off her culinary skills but admitted she has Burnham Market make the cool gazpacho.

Kayaking is now my favourite outdoor activity. I signed on for classes at the Cobourg Canoe Club with three other women. We all love it. We get out on the water two nights a week and paddle around in the bay inside the breakwater. We enjoy the beautiful evenings and good company, including the helpful staff.

Donna with Kayak, Photo by Liz Hammond

Strawberry Fields Forever?
Marie Prins

Recently, I opened a Flickr file of photos, developed from forgotten negatives recently discovered in my mother's basement closet. Childhood memories spilled out, especially one evoked by a photo of myself sitting on a fence post by a farmer's field.

It was 1956, and the summer sun had descended towards distant trees on the western boundary of a vast field. The pickers had left for the day. After a quick surveillance, I climbed the fence separating my backyard from acres of ripe strawberries and scurried out of my mother's sight at the kitchen window. Then I wandered along until I deemed it safe to harvest the plentiful fruit. I squatted in a row and picked berries until they stained my fingers red and filled my belly to bursting. Day after day I partook in this ritual, never bringing a strawberry home, always hoping my mother wouldn't notice the tell-tale signs of my orgies. Truly, she must have, but I cannot remember her displeasure at my obvious greed, only the bountiful blessing of those berries free for the taking.

Decades later, on a June day, I unwittingly found myself partaking in a similar feeding frenzy. I had cut across my neighbour's yard and unleashed my dog to run along the dirt road. Just beyond a hidden creek, another farmer's field stretched to the woods. Its white sign with faded letters "Strawberries – Pick & Pay" pointed towards long rows of ripening fruit. When I neared them, seagulls lifted and cawed their displeasure. With a backwards glance, I bent and located a cluster of ripe berries, skins red and shiny from the night's rain. In seconds, my mouth filled with surplus juice. Chester caught up and ambled down the row to strawberries that tumbled off the plants. I reached into my pocket for the doggie bag and picked two, three berries at a time, discarding ones the gulls had pecked. The bag filled up. I settled on straw next to a cluster of even bigger berries and, one after another, devoured them. Out of the corner of my eye, I glimpsed a fluffy tail dusting weeds a few rows over. Reassured, I ate until I was saturated with fruit. Then I filled a second bag until it barely closed. Satiated and perhaps dazed, I whistled for Chester and we headed slowly home down the dusty road. (For the record, I did pay for those berries.)

Soon strawberry season 2020 will arrive. I wonder how buying or picking this sun-ripened treat will change in this pandemic. No longer having the where-with-all to bend over rows of strawberries, I pray the local farmer's stand will still offer boxes brimming with berries. But will there be pickers to harvest them? Or a friendly face to sell them? Will cash be accepted? Or will I have to order online? Once I pull into the parking lot, will there be lines spacing customers? Or gloved hands depositing pre-paid berries into my trunk? If the farmer wears a mask, will we be able to chat about the weather or the size and sweetness of the berries? Or will it only be a 'hi and bye' exchange?

Wearing a mask to buy strawberries and sanitizing my hands in the car will not be fun. Foregoing the pleasure of immediately popping them into my mouth will definitely be a disappointment. And, to top it off, storing them in the fridge overnight, just in case…will almost be a sacrilege, for as everyone knows, day-old strawberries are not the same. Sigh…such are the times. Hopefully not forever.

Marie on Fence Post, Photo by Harvey Prins

Deer
Antony Di Nardo

I am sitting reading in the giant shadow of Mt. Washington here on its northern side, hundreds of miles away in lockdown, devoted for the moment to the life and thoughts of other people's characters.

I am rummaging through an author's mind as if it was my own, as any reader might do, when my granddaughter calls me from Paris to share a coloured sketch she made in class of four macarons stacked, one on top of the other, like a leaning tower, with one to the side ready to be savoured, so real I can taste it.

She will give the sketch, she tells me, to her grandmother as a birthday gift. Our conversational exchange in our respective confinement takes on the typical phrasings and pauses of characters in a book. *Hmmm*, I say. *Uh-huh*, she says. Our sentences go back and forth like that.

As we are speaking—I am sitting outdoors in a deck chair by a woodland path that leads to the edge of the water—a deer, small but magnificent, saunters out of the woods and comes down for a drink. We watch, stunned into silence (I've flipped the camera on my phone so she can also see it), intent on the beauty before us.

When the deer withdraws with its long, slender legs leaping back into the shadows, my granddaughter tells me, in almost a whisper, of a sketch she recently made of a wolf prowling the woods just behind me. And it's at that point in the story that I catch my breath and pause before I turn the page.

Journal Entry
Antony Di Nardo

The best words are those that reveal nothing.
José Saramago

I spent the summer of 2020 reading and re-reading
Charles Wright and a little of Mary Ruefle.
There is no mystery to the human soul
when the words are right.

I look into the far distance and it ends abruptly,
on the opposite side of the water's edge.
Clouds rim the deep horizon and dip further beyond
where they rest for a while then scatter and shred
and fall to the page.

But what's beyond is not meant to be actually seen,
at least not until I get there myself.
"I hear that the right word will take your breath away."
So says Charles Wright. But which word is it?
For this moment,
this moment right now?

I think it's *murmur*. A murmuring coming from afar.
Let's leave it at that.

Photo by Ann Di Nardo

Benjamin and Dr. Martin Luther King
Diane Taylor

Let me tell you about my son Benjamin and Dr. Martin Luther King, and how I came to write the poem below. And also why I am bringing the poem to light after it has been lying with a collection of other poems in a bottom drawer for the past thirty-seven years, accessible to my eyes only.

Most people come of age in their teens. I came of age during the Civil Rights era of the 1960s. I was well aware of Dr. Martin Luther King's *I Have a Dream* speech when in 1964 I grabbed the chance to march with many others down Yonge Street in Toronto against segregation in Selma, Alabama. Bus-loads of Canadians travelled to Selma to encourage Black voter registration, which had only recently become legal. It was my first year teaching.

In his speech, Dr. King said he could see "One day when little black children would walk hand in hand with little white children…" He was shot and killed in 1968.

In the early 1980s, I had the opportunity to live and work—on a conch farm—in a primarily Black community on a small island in the Caribbean. By then, I was the mother of a one-year-old. It was pure joy for me to see my little white child playing with little black children, living out Martin Luther King's Dream.

In the islands, there was the chance to right the wrongs of the past, to live life the way it should be lived, free from the prejudices of race and colour.

I have a photo of little Ben playing in the sand with his little black friend Nevil. They are both three and a half. The ocean is placid just a few feet away. They are both on their knees, bodies energetically engaged in a fantastic creation, both with their weight on one arm while the other arm is madly pulling sand into a castle that defies archeological logic, but is clearly amazing to both of them. And they had to be fast, for the sun was almost down, on another perfect day, and their mothers would soon be taking them home.

Ben died not long after that photo. A Benless future was unimaginable and unacceptable. Poems were a way of connecting with his spirit and keeping him with me. I shared them with family at the time, but not since. They are too tender a part of me to be casually shared.

Then, George Floyd. After so many others. That's why this is the right time and the right place for the boy named Benjamin to emerge from the bottom drawer into the light.

For Martin Luther King
Diane Taylor

She had a dream
That one day
Her little blond boy
Would walk hand in hand
With little black children.

The dream came to pass
They walked hand in hand
Trekked island paths
Built castles in the sand
Ran Time into the ground.

But, it turns out it's Time
Noncommittal and cold
Does the running
And Time runs out
Into the costly cosmos.

Dr. King? That little blond boy—
Please take his hand in yours.

**Watercolour: Nevil and Ben on the Beach,
Watercolour by Carol Kubie**

Of Babies and Books
Cynthia Reyes

Shall we start with the best part first?

Our grandbaby was christened a few weeks ago. In our garden. Well, on the deck overlooking the garden.

The sun shone warmly, the birds sang a variety of tunes, and the sweet babe, dressed in her beautiful lace christening gown, was secure and placid in her father's arms. Her mother and grandparents beamed with joy while the priest and deacon conducted the sacred ceremony.

The majority of the audience—family members and godparents—attended from afar, by Skype, Zoom and Google Hangout, via laptop computers.

A christening in a garden, attended via the internet? We live in unusual times.

But much of life continues as usual. It's summer and gardening weather—which is not to say I'm gardening much, but that I'm enjoying the sight and sound of the garden. The water in the fountain gently flows. Hummingbirds feed on the red bee balm. Mother and father wren share parenting and housecleaning duties—the hatching and feeding, the nest-cleaning.

Our daughter does a great imitation of a wren, flapping 'wings' and all. She says the phrase 'busy as a bee' should be changed to 'busy as a wren' because these birds never seem to take a break.

To give her parents a break, I take my granddaughter around the garden, pointing out the birds, the flowers, the leaves, the trees and the running water. She looks and listens intently, as if reflecting.

Our potted plants gave me cause for reflection this summer—on how gardening plans can go awry. My colour scheme of yellow, white and blue in one 'room' of the garden was ruined when the yellow canna lilies turned out to be 'coral'—mislabeled. I scowled, then promptly decided to enjoy coral.

Funny—once you get over the early terror of the pandemic, and the intense focus on being safe, you can decide to enjoy this enforced 'staycation.' It helps to note and give thanks for our great privileges— among them reasonably good health, spending time with family, and being in frequent touch with loved ones who live elsewhere.

I am at the stage of deep gratitude.

Small privileges matter too. I stuck with and finished reading a book at last—something I couldn't do while my anxiety was high. A second reading of *Dust* by Martha Grimes.

Reading it this time took so long that I noticed something I hadn't before: the new female police boss, a powerful character of Latin American heritage, was used to spice up Grimes' British murder mystery series—then thrown away in a disappointing *deus ex machina* ending. Worthy of a James Bond movie, perhaps, but I expected better from this author.

Perhaps I also noticed it because the racial injustice leading to the Black Lives Matter protests have made me more reflective these days. I notice things more. Like whose stories are told and valued, whether in monuments or on television.

And who gets thrown away.

It's real life, and it colours even how I read a book.

Real life has a big claim on my time right now. I tinker around the edges of previously written material, but haven't done much book-writing. The time required is better spent with my grandbaby, I know.

The book will still be there—but she is growing so fast and I want to both help her parents and bear witness to her growth.

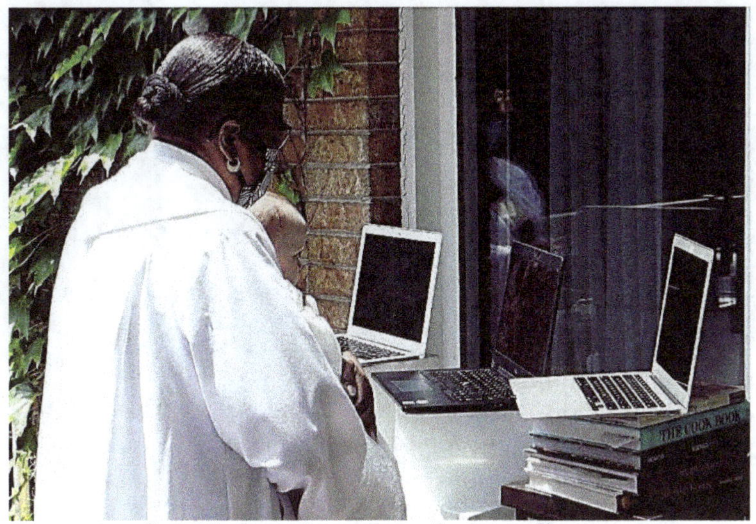

Garden Christening, Photo by Hamlin Grange

Listen
Kim Aubrey

The doe grazing at wood's edge
gazes up as I slow down,
entranced by her calm eyes,
her jaw chewing, her refusal of fear,
the power in her gentleness.

The online teacher invites us to brush
air with palms and soles, to eschew
control's illusion. The yogi advises
watching each thought, making space
for everything that comes.

More gentleness please.
More patience. More listening.
More lightness. More hands held out
to offer help and solace.
More allowing others to be.

Don't let yourself be trampled.
Find the aikido move to spiral out
of harm's way. Treat your opponent
with respect. Don't kill anyone,
or carry a gun, whoever you might be

Find power in stillness, silence. Listen
until it sounds in your body, in the flutter
of your heart, your persistent breath.
Listen until it speaks with none
but your own voice.

Paris Interlude
Christopher Black

She sat quite alone at a sidewalk café,
on a street near the Seine and the Musée D'Orsay,
silver hair shining through the shadows of leaves,
trembling above her, caressed by the breeze,
loves past and lost years, were those tears in her eyes,
when softly she smiled, as one who soon cries,
then picked up her glass of red tinctured wine,
with an elegant hand I wished could touch mine,
and drank again memories of rebellions and art,
as we sat there united, at tables apart.

**Cramahe Hill Cemetery, Photo, Ted Amsden
Photography ©2021**

Gratitude
Katie Hoogendam

Does it seem like everyone is dying?
It does.
And then you realize what a holy miracle
your grandmother's one hundredth birthday was.
In those days, we hugged and our flesh rubbed,
we clinked celebratory glasses of sherbet punch, our
                                       fingers glancing,
and marveled over what a century of life can mean:
two world wars, the invention of cars, a human on the
                                       moon,
plastic and bouffants, cigars,
babies and segregation and Roe v. Wade and the vote,
lipstick and rayon and her camelhair coat.
God, what a mystery, the magic of history,
the fact of our legs in the long grass, the beauty of a body
splayed languidly under a catalpa tree.
So the radio may be off, or you may leave it on.
You see friends from a distance, on the lawn,
wearing bejeweled masks and dropping off surplus
                                       zucchini.
And suddenly, maybe it's the humidity,
the ongoing waves of heat marking total climate calamity
(but we'll save this for another poem)
and you think to yourself, How Marvelous.
Zucchini, jewels on masks, chickens squawking and
                                       prancing,
children the world over leaping through sprinklers like
                                  Swan Lake, dancing,
your grandmother, alive forever in her molasses cookie
                                       recipe—
cookies you could make right now, come to think of it,
because your neighbour bought extra sugar at Costco,
and she dropped it off right on your doorstep, like a gift,
and when you opened the door

in the deep blue of early morning
you were surprised to find a mason jar under shadows, full
of sweet—

just what you needed,
right at your feet.

Something is wrong in the state of—
Shane Joseph

From my cozy writing perch at the cottage window overlooking the deck, I look out upon the gently rolling waters of the lake, protected by its robust treeline comprised of maples, birch, pine, cedar, hemlock and spruce, and I wonder, "Wasn't this the same as when I came here last, in October? The air is nippy as it was then, although the leaves are greener now. But the world was safe then." That world isn't safe now. Not anymore. Not like this peaceful lake is, blissfully unaware at what is causing these humans, who always came to vacation here, to run around with masks on their faces.

Yesterday, America broke out in violence, the pangs of hunger, the lack of social assistance, the unresolved seeds of racism, and the pandemic-induced claustrophobia finally snapping codes of civility. In Canada, provinces began barring residents of other provinces from entering as some were statistically more contaminated with Covid-19, and mask-wearing became de rigueur. "Cover yourselves, so that then we don't need to know who you are or what you represent," it seems to tell me; "A hockey stick's distance is no longer sufficient for my comfort level," it seems to tell me; "Better yet, stay at home for I don't want to see your face again," it tells me.

I'm trying to release a book I wrote during a period of convalescence from a life altering event, one I think would expose the evils of child abuse and fake news, and exalt the power of second chances to redeem. But who the heck wants to read that stuff when we are all living through a common life-altering event? Do people have the time and frame of mind to focus on a full-length book, when the scattershot news-broadcasts appeal more to their shattered concentration? Should fiction writers invent far-off worlds totally removed from this one because everyone just wants to get away?

Talking of getting away, they say travel and tourism will come back in three years. But who the heck can wait around for three years for negative cashflow to turn positive? What is not talked about is that when things open up "gradually" with effective contact tracing, physical distancing, and adequate PPE in place, there is nothing to prevent a member of your staff suddenly receiving a text message to say that they have been identified as being in contact with an "infected one" and needs to self-isolate for 14 days – and, dear boss, you are responsible for compensation and for finding a replacement to cover the absence. The next day, another staff member gets a similar message, Very soon, you are on your lonesome, wishing for a text message yourself so you could shut the place down, or burn it, and vacate for good!

And so I shut off the world and turn to the beloved lake scene in front of me once again. Why spoil these few hours left before I have to return to the real word. Live in the moment, some wise person said, and right now, this moment is precious. For as another wise person said, "it could be worse!"

At the Cottage, Photo by Shane Joseph

Kindness During Covid
Eric E. Wright

Covid-19 means isolation, masks, crowded hospitals and climbing death rates. This is a bad time for all of us. Many face economic catastrophe. Others have had elective surgery postponed. For some surgery or treatment will prove too late. But sprinkled through these days of isolation I see glimpses of kindness.

We live in a condominium complex of four-plex pods, all built on ground level. We have big windows and a front porch giving us prime seats to view life outside our cozy home. Neighbours coming and going. Chatting. Watering their flowers. Bringing home groceries. Walking their dogs. I guess we'd have to admit we've become a bit nosey.

That's why we noticed Reg taking a jug of water with him every evening when he walks his dog. Why? To fill up a dish in the next-door park for all the thirsty dogs who come that way. And we have a lot of dogs from stately Huskies to diminutive Pekinese and quite a few mutts.

And that's how we saw Jan's walker escape her grip and roll across the road. Jan is totally dependent on her walker to take even a step. As she stood there pondering what to do, a neighbour rushed to her aid. He retrieved her walker and proceeded to help her get her groceries from the car. From talking to her we knew it was not easy for her to accept help. She is a self-confessed stubborn Scot.

There's the church that asked its members to write personal cards of encouragement for all the residents of two long-term care facilities, one in Cobourg and one in Port Hope.

Then there's the neighbour who sewed face masks during the early weeks of the crisis. She worked during the day but in the evenings sat down at her sewing machine. She made the finished masks available freely to anyone in the development who could use one. We benefited personally.

And of course, there's Cherie. Cherie loves to talk. She's one of those who once she captures your attention will not stop until she has informed you about her health and past history and any grievances she has with the condo board. As a result, many have taken to giving her a wide berth. Few want to listen for ten or fifteen minutes. Cherie loves flowers and she has created quite an oasis. In spite of her quirks, people have begun to stop and admire her flowers. When she had to be away for a couple of days, one neighbour watered her garden. Now, she can hardly walk, so she has quite a time getting from her condo to the mailboxes. The other day I saw a neighbour holding her arm and helping her home with her mail.

Then there's the grumpy Englishman who is suffering from prostate cancer that has spread into other organs. His prognosis is bad and his appetite much diminished. But he does love eggs, so one neighbour brought him a dozen farm-fresh eggs to enjoy.

We can't forget the neighbours who led a gaggle of us in a social distance singing of O Canada on July first. They arranged it all a couple of days ahead of time, so we could gather in the street outside their condo, while the wife accompanied the rendition on her portable piano. In spite of the gloomy news, we hear each evening, every day we see little acts of kindness taking place outside our picture windows. Neighbours waving and chatting—most at a social distance. It seems as if the corona virus has inspired more neighbourliness! Of course, our community of stubborn Scots, cheery Jamaicans, stolid English, vociferous Poles, and polite Canadians may be unusual. But I doubt it. I can imagine this happening all across Canada.

Front Porch, Photo by Eric E. Wright

Musings
Peggy Dymond Leavey

There's something about being at the cottage that inspires me to put pen to paper. It's always been that way for me, and now, during this 2020 Pandemic Summer, when it's only ever the two of us out here, I feel that urge more strongly.

It could be the absence of any form of social media. With no access to wi-fi I leave my laptop and tablet at home. I don't miss them. They have changed me. I've allowed myself to become distracted by screens. My attention span has shortened, and I find myself flitting between tasks, so that half the time I can't remember what I was doing. I have to force myself to sit and listen to my breathing. Journal writing helps me make sense of my crazy new life.

Over the past 35 years I've done lots of writing out here by the lake. Back in the day when substantive edits to my children's novels arrived in the mail as hard copy from the publisher, I would sit on the deck in the shade of the willows and ponder the editor's suggestions. I love doing revisions. The hard part is already over.

Today is a rainy Sunday with high winds. Long waves pound the rocks on the shore, sending up sheets of spray. Next week some of our family from Pembroke will come to use the cottage for a few days. We haven't seen them since Christmas. We may not see them now. If we are invited to visit we'll have to "social distance" because we are not part of their "bubble." Or should that be their "cohort?"

Our oldest granddaughter, a doctor, will use the cottage again in September while she tours this part of Ontario. We are happy that someone can enjoy this place because we have decided it's time to sell. Maintenance has become increasingly difficult. Our kids loved it out here once, and I hope one day another young family will have the opportunity to do the same.

And I will have to find inspiration in another of nature's quiet corners.

Cottage, Photo by Peggy Dymond Leavey

Focus
Reva Nelson

what makes the most sense
for me to focus on today
should I smell the earth after the
much-needed rain

what about the sight of children
playing separately apart
unsure of whether they can
touch or not

should I listen for the doorbell
even though no one can visit
damn this cursed virus
robbing us of guests

I could touch the beach sand
let it drift through my fingers
warmed by the sun
but it's fenced for safety

the vaccine is coming
we will in time be saved
find meaning in reflection
there's small comfort in the rave

L.B. Welding, Ted Amsden Photography ©2021

Twilight At Almost Full Moon
Ted Amsden

Down by one of the elongated bays
where the roadway slinks through a wetland,
there is a viewing-fishing-passing-by area.

You got some wire fencing,
a sorta smooth asphalt path,
a roadway with rotting guardrails
and down in the water, a culvert
you can paddle through
that allows uptown Northumberland Hills water
to scurry into Lake Ontario.

Fishermen stand on that large road pipe to cast a line.
Families and couples with antsy dogs stop to stare at its
                                    issue.
Geese hump their awkward asses onto land either side.

In the middle of summer, the smooth water that flows from
                                    it
can be impossible to canoe,
the water table cluttered with green-saucer water lilies.

It was twilight the other night,

just finished my bike run to the Lighthouse and back,
ducks of various blends and sizes were on the water,
parked close and far.

Nature's plump white-feathered vegetation vacuums were
upended.

Geese pairs, casual as boaters on a Victorian pond, were
afloat.
Two geese buddies obviously pissed with each other
were butt biting, chest butting and land chasing each other.

Over head the moon was looking very storybook.
Oh, so large and white, with faint age lines.

The sky was that lonesome blue,
fading into darkness soon.

Then I saw him, could be a she,
knew he was in the vicinity,
because there is chicken wire around the bigger trees.
And, there has been sign up since the fall,
tailor-made just for him.

So, not completely unexpected.

But there he was...doing his beaver swimming thing.

Little beaver nose out of the water.
Little beaver face with slicked back fur.
Little V of water ripples spreading out behind him.

I watched him swim as he followed the shoreline
like my brother in his fancy boat does when he's out just
lookin'.

Pulling in tight for a closer view,
maybe to see if there is any beaver value at water's edge,
he resumed course at a distance.

Perhaps, he was just on his evening rounds of the
                                    neighbourhood.

And as he became smaller and smaller the further from me,
I found myself in a familiar reverie,
asking what guides creatures?

I find it difficult to believe
that they are simply natural machines
operating within the system of nature to
visual and physical prompts engineered by genetic
                                    programming.

Sometimes a creature symphony in front of me,
like this tableau of birds and beaver framed by a gentle
                                    Spring evening,
transcends itself and teases me.

Evolution doesn't have all the answers.

Bird in Tree, Ted Amsden Photography ©2021

Memoir or Short Story—A Creative Decision Made During Pandemic
Michael Croucher

I've been toying with the idea of writing my memoirs for a while now. But I've always written fiction, and memoirs present challenges to the *what-if* mindset of fiction writers. Memoirs are factual, with elements of fancy used very carefully. That's a tall order because we rely on dialogue and vivid description to advance our plots. Also, remembering exactly what occurred, or what was said in the past is often difficult, if not impossible, and the temptation to polish up dialogue, descriptions and characters is strong. Most fiction writers need to pull their readers along by building interest, so the temptation to fictionalize memoir becomes very powerful. I've decided to avoid the temptation, I'm going to utilize my creative liberties and treat my memoir material as fiction; change names and alter situations where needed.

I've had plenty of time to read during the lockdown, and a piece of the late Alistair MacLeod's writing helped me make this decision. He addressed this dilemma in a notation at the start of a short story, "To Every Thing There Is a Season," one of my favourites, a beautifully written piece.

He wrote in the notation, "yet when I speak (of the past), I am not sure how much I speak with the voice of that time or how much in the voice of what I have since become. And I am not sure how many liberties I may be taking with (who) I think I was...For both past and present...are often imperfectly blended. As we step into nowness we often look behind." MacLeod nailed it.

I will still write and keep a private copy of my *non-fictionalized* memoirs, but I'm fictionalizing some of them. That way, I'll have more short-story material, and I'll be free to tell the stories in a way that has a better chance to entertain readers, and hopefully compel them to read on. I'll always have plenty to write about. I wonder if writers occasionally suffer from writer's block because they're seeking inspiration from the outside. They ignore the inspirational treasure boxes within: experiences, memories and an imagination that is not compromised by fear of crossing the line between fiction and memoir.

Ode to Summer
Donna Wootton

On the porch in the shade visiting
sitting on a wicker chair
a cyclist passes
black spandex shorts
yellow top

Never again will I click my feet into cleats!

Hostess agrees.
she, too, broke her ankle recently
hence the visit to commiserate
broke mine in 2017

We share recovery details

Isn't it fortunate her break happened
at the start of COVID-19?
motivated to stay home she had help,
a sister visiting,
a son working from home

Always good can be found in everything.

We went to the same clinic out-of-town
It was open during the emergency closure

Both in an air cast can walk but she had surgery
mine was a clean break bone mended
muscles atrophied

Breeze cools...don't stay long
her ankle swelling...give her a rest

We'll meet again.

Walk home along the shaded sidewalk
look what I see...
a red canoe
a yellow kayak
a wraparound porch
a corner garden
purple clematis
someone walking a dog skinny legs on pet and owner
Don't break a leg!

Two women laughing
another porch visit
this is the town for them
beautiful porches built a century ago
before air conditioning

So much nicer to be outside than shut-up indoors.

Porch, Photo by Donna Wootton

The Proverbial Veil Has Lifted
Linda Hutsell-Manning

Arriving home in March from an idyllic ten days in rural Costa Rica to quarantine and this relatively closeted life required a substantial mental and emotional shift. Before Covid, my memoir, *Fearless and Determined,* was selling exceptionally well with fifteen readings booked between March and October. All now cancelled. I rationalized and hoped that, in a few months, normalcy would return. As we all know, this has not happened.

Without consciously deciding, writing simply stopped being a priority. With spring approaching, our country property provided ample yard work as well as exercise I was missing at the Y.

One bright spot appeared. In April, my niece, Program Co-ordinator at a Toronto Seniors' Centre, asked me to give a Zoom reading to her afternoon group. Talking and reading about my memoir proved so successful that subsequently each month, I have given readings. Each time, during that one hour, I felt like a writer again. One day a month, however, could not sustain my writing zeal. I returned to yard work and, more recently, an accumulated-belongings purging in our century home.

Several years ago, our Naturopath son, David, said he would move back to live in our house and look after us. "No old people's home for you," he had said vehemently. Subsequently, he and our daughter bought our place and David will return permanently in May 2021.

Since then, we have been cleaning out the third-floor storage room for his bedroom, with the west bedroom for his office. The storage room, containing forty-five years of stuff, must be empty by March to start renovations. I have been ploughing through endless forgotten things: boxes of children's elementary and high school work; a heavy cardboard box containing a grade eleven architecture project complete with plaster of Paris base, house, garage and pool, all landscaped and mouse-eaten; tinker toy and Meccano; too many old suitcases, framed pictures, bed frames and four old trunks, one containing seventy year-old tap-dancing and ballet costumes for children's dress up; a plywood sheet with a train track, mouse-eaten trees and landscaping; several antique non-functioning lamps; outdated computer hardware and software from our closed computer store. And the list goes on. It brings to mind Plum Johnson's delightful book, *They Left us Everything*. I would retitle it, *We Left Ourselves Everything!*

By mid-July, major furniture moving and room reorganizing was complete. My office included my grandmother's beautiful, old three-drawer desk. The storage room was half empty; we sold some unwanted things; recycled seven boxes of clothing; moved furniture and reorganized bookcases.

This abruptly changed, however, August first weekend. I felt as though a proverbial veil lifted; a door opened; I was a writer again.

Appearing at Let's Talk Books was the catalyst. I didn't expect to sell books, but just being there and chatting with people made me feel like a writer. The amazing thing was I sold six memoirs and one picture book!

Over a hundred Facebook friends responded to the report of my event, many with positive comments. With readings cancelled and few sales, this was such a boost. Emails and letters continue to praise my memoir, some who remember, others fascinated with its social history. This spurs me on.

I now have three projects in mind: a memoir about my unorthodox childhood and equally unlikely road to becoming a writer and two grandmother-related historical fiction possibilities.

Given I'll be eighty in a few days, I'd better get writing!

Clouds over County Road 25,—Ted Amsden Photography ©2021

Sleeping Cat
Gwynn Scheltema

a waterfall of sleeping cat
spills from my lap
his purr thrumming through my thigh
up to my heart
a comfortable heaviness
this curl of cat
rising and falling
with each breath I take
each low hum of purr
a sleep song of
heart harmonies

Cats on Lap, Photo by Gwynn Scheltema

New Life in the Midst of Lockdown
Janet Stobie

The Pandemic and lockdown brought life to a halt for much of the world. For me, the last four months have been built around change and new life. For sure, opportunities for speaking and selling my books totally dried up. Since that has always been my primary market, I just took a deep breath and shelved that part of my life. The space remained empty for four weeks. April 6 our first great grandson arrived one month early. Since his parents live with us, he joined our bubble. New life in the midst of Covid-19. We are truly blessed. I have cuddled and rocked and sang, while our beautiful baby Riley slept like an angel. Now he plays and smiles and laughs. It won't be long before he crawls, and our lives will change yet again.

Using mostly early morning time, I've worked on two writing projects. Writing and rewriting my children's picture book story, *Rajah Becomes a True King*, filled my early morning hours for two months. At this point Rajah has been professionally edited by Jennifer Rees. Illustrator Malabika Saikia is now creating the pictures. Publication date is planned for November 10.

Thanks to Covid-19 I may give birth to twins. Not human babies but my book babies. I've been writing monologues reflections on scripture stories for the last five years. Two weeks ago, I sent them off to professional editor Ruth Walker. The collection will be called *Celebration Stories*. Publication date is planned for November 10. Obviously, this set of twins are fraternal.

As things open up I'm discovering that my life is picking up speed. I'll need to plan a virtual book launch and blog tour. Both are brand new experiences for me. I am truly grateful that my life is full.

Janet and Riley

Letter from Jack to his Mom
Patricia Calder

May 28th, 1941
Dear Mom,

You would have loved flying with me today. We are nearing the end of our flight training, so we had a more or less free day to fly over northern England and even into Scotland and Wales, in a big circle. Each country is so different from the others. England has miles and miles of tiny green fields surrounded by hedge rows, villages each with its church spire + school + post office + of course the local pub. Wales is remarkable for its dark mountains where the coal miners make their living. Even the towns have a dark tone, I suppose from the coal dust. The poverty is evident from the air. Scotland, on the other hand, is refreshingly colourful. Its mountains are covered with green hills inviting one to go hiking. I'm planning a holiday there the next time I'm on leave.

Bob and I are sharing a room and training together. We have a small coal stove in the middle of the room which keeps the hut fairly comfortable. We often share mugs of tea late at night sitting around the stove before bed. In fact, that's where I am now, so you can picture me. I'm in the peak of health as I'm sure we are served the best bacon and eggs in the country. The meals in the mess are hearty and we are given lunch packs to take on each trip if we are going to be away for hours. Our laundry is done for us, even ironing and boot polishing; whereas the NCO's must do their own, poor sods! It's worth being an officer in this war, I'm telling you. My university education is paying off in that respect at least.

Some of the boys over here have serious girlfriends back home, and some are getting into serious relationships over here. Mom, I have decided not to pledge any promises to a girl until the war is over. It probably won't last too long and I can wait for some kind of normal to return. When we go on leave I just want to be light hearted and have fun. I don't want any girl pining for me while I'm on ops; that wouldn't be fair, in my opinion. I know other fellows think differently. They want to live it up and experience love because they might not live to see tomorrow, but I am optimistic that my future will be bright once we give Gerry a good knock-out punch. This is just a job we have to get done first.

Our training officers are great. They all have experience on ops so they know what they're talking about. I'm learning so much every day. Bob is a wonderful pilot. He and I make a superb team, together with the other 5 in our crew. They are great lads all and we're becoming friends as well as mates. We look out for each other. Sorry that this letter is wandering all over the place but it's been a long day, even though an exhilarating one of a long practice flight. I navigated well enough to touch all points on the map we were supposed to and get us back to the aerodrome in time for supper. Bob sends best wishes to you and Dad. He promises to bring me home safely so try not to worry.

Love to all,

Jack

Jack © Patricia Calder

In the Hills of Appalachia
Antony Di Nardo

Big ideas coming down from the hills
               and bigger yet I get lost among the leaves,
that cool green element in the upper Appalachians.

Big trees get bigger every day
               and yet somehow never linger forever.
Same goes for the folk in the valley.

Bye-bye lilies, it's the last of you today, gone to God
                         knows where.
The pretty pinks have also gone
               and the banjo-picking peepers.

A few words can make everything so real.

One less lily and the impossible iris of yesterday is now
                  in a world of its own.

There are some reflections only I can see
                 and some only when
           the light's turned on, as it is
at this very moment,
     green right through in the hills of Appalachia.

Photo by Ann Di Nardo

Imagine
Antony Di Nardo

that the sun has yet to leave
   and it's almost at the point of no return
that time of day when the lake's not as lively
  and the sheen of its watery lustre is dimming.

Lilies are beginning to fall apart, the shrapnel of petals
   in a soft explosion.

The old ways of doubling up are vanishing for now,
  the water's surface a blank that keeps you guessing
what's real and what was once in deep reflection.

Trees are losing their sight
   and the big green spaces diminishing,
flattened in the persistent gloaming,
    green to dark green
then black as blindness hovering below the withering
   until there's nothing left to see but darkness,
tight as a fist.

The old ways may be changing—the absence of light
    marks the end of the lilies,
but whatever you imagine beyond today
   that might come tomorrow
    was here before.

The Chair
Felicity Sidnell Reid

The chair had always been substantial,
found abandoned in a run-down property,
destined to become their family home.
Both demanded restoration of their dignity and grandeur.

In her father's house it was his chair,
the undisputed seat of dominance,
whence he surveyed his shrinking kingdom,
as age and illness left him beached on it.

He sat, a stony idol, dark eyes flickering,
in his white face, crowned by silvery hair.
And when he died, she took it by default
since no-one else could find a use for it.

But where to put it? A little shabby now:
the crimson velvet rubbed, the stuffing holding
firm an old man's shape, that now she
understands was the most personal
legacy she could receive from him.

She hauls the chair to the window
that overlooks her garden. Its cushioned arms
console her as she settles in its warm embrace.
It will be my chair now, she thinks, watching her cat
drawn towards sunshine, braced to leap into her lap.

A Cog in The Machine
Alan F. Bland

"What are these," I said as the young lad from the mailroom put several large packages on my desk.

"Don't know, but they come every month, I was told. And to give them to you," he said, turning and walking away.

I had just taken over the desk from old Jones, who had retired, but he'd not warned me that stacks of strange forms would suddenly appear, or what I was expected to do with them. I finished what I had been doing, which was a task that seemed to have no purpose, pushed those papers aside and took hold of the first bundle. Then reconsidered. No need to jump right in, when I could go for a stroll to the kitchen and pour another coffee.

While there I was joined by a few other paper-pushers, all of whom were engaged in equally meaningless tasks that were somehow expected to benefit the country as a whole and mankind in general. Or at least that's what we had all been told when we joined Section 3 of Department D.

After the mandatory discussion of the weather and which hockey and baseball teams would make the play-offs we all migrated back to our identical pods in the pod-farm.

Feeling that it was time to start I picked up the top multi-page form and looked for a title; some clue that would tell me its purpose and possibly what the next step on its journey would be. Aha! It's a K dash 73 stroke 99, version X dash 17, part 12, it told me. Maybe there's something more on the last page, I thought. Nothing appeared there so I flicked through all seven pages and found nothing that shed any light on what I was holding in my hand, or what to do with it.

Looking over the pages one-by-one I could see that it was a computer-generated form with multiple choices answered by picking a number's corresponding dot from 1 to 10. But the questions didn't accompany the answers. So if all this information was stored in a computer somewhere why were these forms printed off? And what was I to do with them? I asked a few of my neighbour pod-dwellers if they had ever come across a K dash 73 stroke 99, version X dash 17, part 12, before, but nobody had.

I thought the best thing to do would be to back-track the packages through the mailroom and set off to find who had put them into the system. After moving from department to department it seemed as if an elaborate game of pass-the-parcel was going on, until in a dark corner of a basement file room I came upon an area walled in by stacks of file boxes with a slim opening next to the wall. And here I found the source of those mysterious forms. There was an old Steelcase desk with the oldest IBM computer I had ever seen and the dot-matrix printer that had spewed out those forms.

Over the years the file boxes had absorbed smoke from countless cigarettes and maybe some other form of indulgence. Although smoking had long been banned in office buildings the odour still lingered, along with a musty smell of damp and dust. The boxes on the lower tiers were crushed and sagging and I doubt had been opened in years, if not decades.

Seated at the desk a pony-tailed man with John Lennon glasses was tapping time to music coming to him via headphones from an old cassette player. Once I got his attention, he seemed shocked to see me before him. Reluctantly he turned off the music and removed the headphones.

"I wonder if you can tell me anything about these," I said handing him a sample.

"No-one ever comes down here," he said in response, distrust evident from his tone.

"Look I just want to know what to do with them," I said.

He looked distressed. "Nothing, don't do anything with them. Please."

"But what are they for? And why do we need them?" I asked.

"I don't know. I've just been printing them off for years. Look, no-one remembers I'm down here. My pay goes into the bank every month and one day I'll quietly retire. I'm just a part of the system, another cog in the machine. I suspect that old Jones just put them through the shredder. If I don't keep doing this they won't need me anymore, and I'll be terminated."

I looked around at his little corner in the system, at being just another cog in the machine.

"Well then you'd best keep sending them," I said and went back to my own little corner of the system, to being just another Cog-in-the-Machine.

Brighton Gas Bar, Photo—Ted Amsden Photography ©2021

FALL 2020

Photo by Ann Di Nardo

The Ups and Downs of Lockdown
Michael Croucher

Being mostly confined to home for the last eight months has been tough. Like everyone, we miss seeing our kids, our grandkids, and the grand pets (3 dogs, 1 cat). We have good days and bad days. Fortunately the bad days are short-lived. We keep busy. It's easy to get down at times though. We're social creatures, for God's sake. We're not meant to be cut off.

We got through the first wave. Now we're bracing for a second go-round. But we know what to expect. This time we'll venture out a bit more with a good understanding of how to protect ourselves and our loved ones. Hope it goes well.

Writers are loners, stand-offish creatures by reputation. We crave human contact. Though we rarely get in people's faces, we need to be around them for entertainment, inspiration and appreciation. The absence of those things feels especially bad for those of us who are dragging our backsides into dotage.

There were some silver linings to the lockdown: more time to write, more time to think, more time to reflect—start new projects. I've dabbled with memoir. Not to publish, just to write. I'll create print-on-demand copies for loved-ones and friends. I try to be honest, revealing my warts to all. There has been an offsetting bonus to writing memoirs: great ideas for my fiction. I'm happy to share a piece of a memoir on this blog:

I enjoyed school. I was never a good student. Far from it. I got in the odd scrap, but didn't start them. In those days, you stood up for yourself or you kept paying the price. I was a restless kid, didn't apply myself to subjects I had no interest in. My attitude was another concern. Eventually I was shown the door.

It was 1961. I joined the RCAF with my parents' consent. They had to sign for me because I was under 18. They were both ex-

military (my dad RAF, my mom WAAF). I went to boot camp in St. Jean Quebec; three tough months, but I really enjoyed them.

Things went downhill from there. After boot camp and the graduation parade, they lined my group up in a hangar, separated us, and assigned half to electronics school at RCAF Clinton and the other half to radar school at Falconbridge. No aptitude testing that I remember. Another parade, and we were on a train to Clinton.

My military career lasted almost a year. When I flunked electronics—no aptitude for technology then or now—I was sent up to the Commanding Officer for an interview. He offered me a trade switch: bartender, cook, or air force policeman.

John Diefenbaker was Prime Minister then. He'd just introduced an austerity programme to cut military spending. When I turned down the transfers, the C.O. said he would discharge me if I went back to school. I said I would. I didn't.

Within two months I'd been accepted as a Police Cadet in Toronto and was starting my motorcycle training. I was in a better place.

Thank you, Prime Minister Diefenbaker. I did go back to school as a mature student, took business courses at the University of Toronto whenever my shifts allowed.

Throughout the pandemic, I've applied the air force motto. *Per Ardua ad Astra*—through adversity to the stars. That, the company and support of my wife of 52 years, enough space in the house for both of us, and my writing, have kept my spirits up.

Photo by Ann Di Nardo

The First Days of World War Two
Maureen Mullally

On September 6th 1939, I was 6 years old.

Gillian asked me to play. She lived across the road and sometimes cars went by, so Mummy said I had to be very careful crossing. Gillian had lots of dolls, but they weren't as nice as mine. I told her they needed a wash. She didn't like that and we started to quarrel. Suddenly a loud wailing noise came from outside. Mr. West, Gillian's Daddy, hurried into the room and said it was a siren and he would take me home. I was frightened and wanted Mummy. I tried to wiggle my arm away from Mr. West. After we crossed the road, I said, "Goodbye, thank you for having me." I was still trying to wiggle out of his grip, but he held tight until Mummy came running and took me inside. She told me war had broken out and the noise was air raid sirens. They were still wailing up and down. The grownups were all talking at once—nobody knew what we should do. Daddy said now we were at war with the Germans, we should 'take cover' in the garage. He moved the car out and took deck chairs into the empty garage. We all put on our coats and Wellington boots. Our neighbours, Mr. and Mrs. Gardiner and their son Victor, came as well. Nothing seemed to be happening after the sirens stopped. Eventually we went inside and had our tea.

But many changes were about to happen.

Street lights were unlit and house lights had to be 'blacked out' with curtains, so no light showed in the streets. Dad made boards instead of curtains to prevent possible shattered glass. Air Raid Wardens patrolled to make sure no light was showing. Street signs were removed. Pig-bins were installed on every street, as household vegetable waste was diverted to help feed farm animals. We were issued gas masks in cardboard boxes attached to a cord to wear over our shoulders. We had to take them with us wherever we went. Ration books were issued to buy meat, eggs, butter, cheese and canned goods.

Other food was in very short supply, except for vegetables. Unbleached flour made pale brown bread. We all longed for proper white bread! Park land was taken over to grow food and divided into allotments. Everyone was encouraged to plant their own vegetables, to 'Dig for Victory,' as the billboards told us.

The government had prepared an evacuation scheme to get as many children as possible out of London and other cities. Trains and buses took thousands of children to be billeted in the country. I remember pictures in the paper of hundreds of bewildered children, some just toddlers with their names on labels attached to their coats, at bus stops and railway stations, while crying parents waved goodbye.

My Mother would have nothing to do with any of that. She had an alternative idea.

A private school was going to Wales. Mum finagled an arrangement which let me be included with a neighbour's daughter, who would look after me. She wasn't keen to have an unhappy little kid with a white Teddy Bear trailing after her and did her best to lose and ignore me. I was told to sleep on a crumpled pile of covers on the floor. I remember lying on the itchy straw mattress, crying. Fortunately, Mum got news of the poor conditions and dispatched Dad in short order to bring me home.

When Mrs. Gardiner and her family rented a house in the country, she persuaded Mum to let me go with them, so off I went. I attended school but it was very strange. Children wrote on slates, and some of them stayed there at night. But Mrs. Gardiner took us to the beach most days after school and made raspberry jam sandwiches for tea. The big earthenware pot of jam lasted forever and inevitably sand got mixed with the sandwiches. I slept on a camp bed in Mrs. Gardiner's room. When she came to bed, I was often awake, intrigued to watch her remove her corsets, scratching herself with relief. Goodness knows why she wore corsets; she was thin as a rake. I demonstrated this activity to Mummy when I returned home, much to her amusement.

I was quite happy during my stay there, but after three months we all returned home.

Maureen's House, 'La Paque,' 52 The Ridgeway, Waddon, England

Thanksgiving Dinner, 2020
Felicity Sidnell Reid

Zooming in on steaming food
set out on pretty plates,
we eye each other's offerings,
recall advice from earlier years,
"Watch out, your eyes are
bigger than your belly!"
No problem this year
as we cannot reach to taste
but only wonder at
my daughter's lentil bake
swaddled in a puffy golden coat
surrounded by the last
green greens and red tomatoes
from her overflowing garden.
My son shows us
his heaping bowl of rice
studded with nuts and fruit
bursting with multicoloured
vegetables and all admire it.
I pay homage to their vegan
principles with a plate
of sweet potato curry,
rice and yet more salad.
We raise our glasses wishing
each other *Happy Thanksgiving*,
grateful we can see and talk,
even engage in similar
if separate actions.
Silently, we dream of next
year, hoping we'll share
the cooking and the food—
together.

Fall of squirrels
Kim Aubrey

This fall our squirrels are fatter than God.
Nourished by this generous land,
they hold worlds in their bellies.

Maples offer outstretched limbs
for the squirrels' high-wire acts,
brilliantly executed feats of daring.

For now they continue light on their feet,
can run the length of a power line,
scale a roof, but when will the extra

weight they're packing keep them
from leaping? What is the tipping point
where health turns into harm

where flight takes a fall? Will they evolve
into ground squirrels, leave branches
to sway empty above?

My mother's town has a surfeit of squirrels;
a long summer has supplied an extra
breeding cycle. Their corpses spatter
highways and parking lots.

But our squirrels are not at locust capacity.
Instead of multiplying their species,
they've opted to multiply their cells,
grow their own rotund bellies.

More tempted to feed than to mate,
unconcerned about preserving the species,
they've become self-preserving.

Basic needs cared for, they learn new arts,
lounge and play and savour, tend
to their burgeoning inner lives.

A Grandparent's Wonder and Anxiety
Cynthia Reyes

I stare at my grandchild in wonder.

Wonder at this little person who, at eleven months old, already has a personality of her own. She stands up from a sitting position, starts to wobble, but regains her balance. When she falls, she lifts herself up and stands again, beaming.

Her mother and I applaud.

"What a sweet child," I tell my daughter. "I can't believe how fast she's growing."

She smiles in agreement.

I hope my granddaughter will grow up healthy and well. That she will always feel loved. That she will care for others, not just herself. That she will do well in school and work. That one day she will find a good partner and have children of her own. I hope for all this.

But anxiety sometimes creeps in as I watch her trying to walk, holding on to the furniture or standing on her own. Anxiety that she will fall. And an even bigger worry.

What will have happened to humanity by the time my granddaughter has children of her own?

What kind of world will they inherit?

Will nations continue to split along ideological lines? Will we humans continue to express hatred for each other across those lines? Will the US, where many of my own relatives live, fight a civil war, complete with guns?

In my own networks, I've seen what happens when people choose power over reconciliation. When they attack, instead of talking. When they choose to bully others, instead of seeking a way forward together.

And what will have happened to the planet by the time my granddaughter has her own grandchildren? Will humans, while squabbling with each other, have killed off the wildlife, irretrievably damaged the air we breathe, the water we drink and the soil that grows our food?

"Ah, Cynthia," I stop and chide myself. "You're a bunch of chuckles today. Give it a rest."

My daughter catches the strange look on my face and asks, "What are you thinking?"

I tell her a softened-up truth. I say: "I'm hoping my granddaughter will have a good life. And that the Earth will be in good shape for her and her children."

She looks at me, thoughtful, then lunges to stop her baby from grabbing an object from a shelf.

"Another part of the house to baby-proof," we both say knowingly.

Becoming a grandparent is similar and different to parenting. A friend, grandmother of seven children, tells me, laughing: "The great thing is that you can send them home to their parents!"

But priorities change. Though I'm not the parent, the tasks that took priority—even writing—are now in second or third place when my daughter and son-in-law need my help.

Having grandchildren also makes me think about longevity. Will I be around when she's an adult? Will I get to meet her children—or is that too much to ask?

The longevity and wellbeing of the planet are also on my mind. What do my privileged aspirations matter if high temperatures, flooding, hurricanes and wildfires make life impossible for much of humanity?

"Give it a rest," I repeat, silently, and return to playing with my granddaughter, pledging to stay with her in the moment.

She lives entirely in the present: turning the pages of a favourite book, banging a wooden spoon against a box.

She crawls up the stairs more swiftly and confidently each day, and races me across the floor, laughing as I tease: "No fair! You're an expert at crawling, and I'm not!"

She pulls items from her toy basket, throwing them on the floor around her. I refill the basket. She throws them out again and beams with achievement. "The sorting phase," I'm told.

I stare at her in wonder and allow myself to banish the worry – at least for today.

VV and Grandma
Photo by Lauren Reyes-Grange Leca

Wanted: A Balanced Forum for Debate
Shane Joseph

I belonged to my high school debating society a long time ago, a place I loved to hang out for ideas and intellectual stimulation. Anything and everything was debatable in those days, as long as we followed the rules of debating: make your case, let the other side make theirs, and sum up. Then debrief, extract the learning, and share it with everyone. And always show respect for the opposition, for without them there would be no debate.

That form of debating carried into my adult life. When I read newspapers, there were always opposing viewpoints juxtaposed on the same page; journalists featured both sides of the coin in their articles. Even the so-called left-leaning or right-leaning magazines had limited opposing views for contrast. Television featured multiple viewpoints in debates and discussions, and the same occurred in newscasts and talk shows.

Over the last ten years, I have seen that diversity of viewpoint erode. Everyone has taken up a position and sticks to it, and wants their audience to think like them as well. The newspapers and TV news channels have polarized, and identify as either right wing or left wing. If you tune in to CNN or Fox News you know pretty much what you are in for. The same goes with the Toronto Star vs. the Toronto Sun.

It got worse after social media went mainstream and the "like and share" culture was born. Partisanship became fashionable. For how could you get the maximum "likes" and "shares," if the audience didn't like or share your view? "Echo chamber" entered the vernacular. And the fickleness of social media—where you could be deleted from "friendship" at the disenchanted click of a button—made it difficult to address thorny issues to a diverse audience; someone was likely to get incensed and delete you.

When I think of the arms-length relationship that once existed between the four estates—legislature, executive, judiciary and press—

and between them and the barons of commerce, this symbiosis created balanced debate involving multiple viewpoints. The erosion of independence between these bodies over time, has caused the resulting polarization. In many jurisdictions today, even in the ones that were proudly founded upon the separation of powers, the executive has tended to subsume the other estates, and the corporate barons in turn seem to have subsumed the executive. Now we have those *in* power vs. those *without*, and they change colours with every election cycle; debate has now been reduced to one side shouting at the other—didn't we see that at the recent Presidential Debate, an example set by the highest office?

Does another Age of Enlightenment need to dawn before we can re-develop honest debate? Or could social media companies restructure their huge membership bases to demolish echo chambers and replace them with productive debating forums? As for newspaper and TV companies that complain about shrinking viewership, could they look beyond their narrow partisan bases to broader ones that embrace all sides of an issue? This utopian thinking flies in the face of "market segmentation" that all media companies strive to maximize, in order to operate at a profit. But if media is in the broader business of disseminating knowledge via the exchange of ideas, then it needs to realize that a diversity of opinions is what is valued and not the narrow targeting of a right or left-wing echo chamber.

In the meantime, I continue to seek out honest souls to have an intelligent debate with—unfortunately, I won't find them in the usual places.

Swan, Photo by Shane Joseph

Myrtle and the Big Mistake
Cynthia Reyes

Just before the pandemic hit Canada, my book-writing partner Lauren and I pulled out our chairs and sat at the harvest table. Its surface gleams with age and polish, a rich, medium brown, 7 feet long. Its legs are sturdy and old-fashioned.

Around this table, we eat our meals, sometimes the big traditional meals like birthday and Thanksgiving dinners. This harvest table is as Canadian as maple syrup—made from thick planks of maple wood for a Masonic lodge more than a century ago.

It's where we create every sequel to the first Myrtle the Purple Turtle book which I wrote nearly thirty years ago for Lauren when she was almost 5 years old.

Lauren's a mother now. Her husband holds their baby daughter as we brainstorm. A yellow foolscap writing pad is in front of me. Lauren mulls the storyline of this book we want to write about a talkative parrot who spreads a false rumour.

It's become a tradition: we don't leave the harvest table till we've figured out the storyline.

Our readership. we've learned, ranges from 3 to 10 years old. The storyline and pictures must be simple enough to engage the youngest readers, with themes meaty enough to attract older ones.

Next, we turn the storyline into a story, with beginning, middle and end. As with books for adults, there has to be a hook, a problem to solve, actions taken to overcome the challenges, and a resolution.

Lauren and I hammer out the first draft and send it to Jo, our illustrator.

"It's a first draft, Jo," we always tell her. "Just sharing the storyline. We're not there yet."

Jo, who loves Myrtle, won't wait for the final edit, however. As always, she starts illustrating.

She asks if there's a final title. Lauren and I are stuck. We ask Hamlin (my husband) who is usually good at titles, but none of us can find one we all like.

The pandemic hits, and priorities change. We're frantically ordering groceries online then washing off each item as it arrives. We sow seeds for spinach and herbs indoors. We worry about relatives and friends.

We email Jo in South Africa, not about the book, but about the safety of her family. She writes back, enquiring about ours and telling us her family is healthy so far.

Spring gets underway.

This time, we're waiting for the editor in England to recommend changes to the manuscript before it's sent to an international group of beta readers—children, parents, grandparents and teachers.

We send Jo an update, asking for patience.

An American teacher enquires: Is there a discussion guide for the 3 earlier Myrtle books?

Oops—we'd discussed this earlier but forgotten. We set to work again.

The books are used by some child psychologists. Luckily, we know someone in that profession. She reviews both manuscript and discussion guide.

Next, we send the whole draft to all the beta readers.

"Please hang in there, Jo!" I email meanwhile. "We're waiting to hear back from beta readers!"

The suggestions are in. Someone—I forget who—suggests we make the names in the book more international—so we sit at the harvest table and struggle through that. I love Francesca for a girl character—but Lauren thinks it's a bit difficult to say. We change it.

"And what about the final title?" Jo asks.

Title? Oh dear. More brainstorming. We settle on one of the first titles suggested.

"Myrtle and the Big Mistake!" We tell Jo.

The illustrations are in and all should be well, when Hamlin discovers 3 omissions in the text. We edit again, begging Jo's forgiveness.

Myrtle and the Big Mistake is published three months later. It's a beautiful book.

Sitting at the harvest table again, we celebrate.

Harvest Table, Photo by Cynthia Reyes

Radio Classique Montréal
Antony Di Nardo

I'm out of sorts
and I want to use the word *penumbra*
in a sentence—
there I've said it—
I was reading Brautigan all day yesterday
and "Girl" is the title of that Beatles' song
I just remembered
and I remember too
bushels of apples
pecks of Muscatel grapes
quarts of being indisposed
the cool dips and ponds of dear Quebec
your back to me
my back to you
and you don't have to be infected
to be affected
crackling out of the radio at 7 a.m.
the first words I hear today
while thinking
I love your back
to mine

Anniversaries
Mia Burrus

August 6 and 9 are the 75th anniversaries of the atomic bombing of Hiroshima and Nagasaki. I am rereading John Hersey's account of six hibakusha, literally "explosion-affected persons," thinking of the tiny lanterns set afloat on the river each August, and the Hiroshima memorial/museum, which, if I had a bucket list, would be on it.

I made a point of completing another anniversary project this week, one I started just after New Year, about the 30th anniversary of the Montreal Massacre, whose date was December 6, 2019. This anniversary of an event which happened in my lifetime became the thorn on the red rose, useless repetition, regression, the record with a skip in it. It started as a poem but devolved into an assemblage, finally becoming a setting for a 'poem' (or the world's shortest play). I literally stick it to the white ribbon campaign, with side trips into Atwood's *The Handmaid's Tale* and Greek tragedy. I have tried to remain positive! **Res ipse loquitur.**

Montreal Massacre
Mia Burrus

Dramatis Personae

The Fates, robed in white,
whom Erebus begot on Night:

Clotho : *with spindle and loom and white
linen thread*
Lachesis : *unspooling ribbon with a
measuring rod*
Atropos: *small and terrible, wielding shears*

Chorus of Women: *heard from the distant
land of the dead*
Priestesses of Hestia: *tending the embers,
gift of their god*
Suppliant Women: *terribly small, hiding
their tears*

Mute: the rifle-maker, the soap-box builder,
the brooding recluse

A winter night, lit by the moon
The Chorus sings basso continuo: *weave*   *draw*   *cut*
pin

Clotho: I spin the sacred strands of my own self and weave
them into cloth that is fine and pure, endowed with all that
is divine.

                         weave   *draw*   *cut*   *pin*
Lachesis: I draw web-delicate lengths of ribbon, read with
fingers fine and pure the life unfurled, imperfect, yes, and
in places rough.

weave   draw   cut   pin

Atropos: I execute a cut, my silver blade so fine and pure a lightning strike in darkest night.

weave   draw   cut   pin

Suppliant Women: We pin the ribbons, wipe our tears, and pin again, against the pain, sacrifice the captured small white butterflies, surrender our dead sisters to the page, that we be free to turn, to wholly occupy the stage.

weave   draw   cut   pin

Priestesses: Majestic women, immeasurable as flame! You carry within you our sacred blaze.   But do not settle for remembrance and release. Hestia's embers burn eternal and for eternal peace.

Exeunt: the rifle-maker, the soap-box builder, the brooding recluse

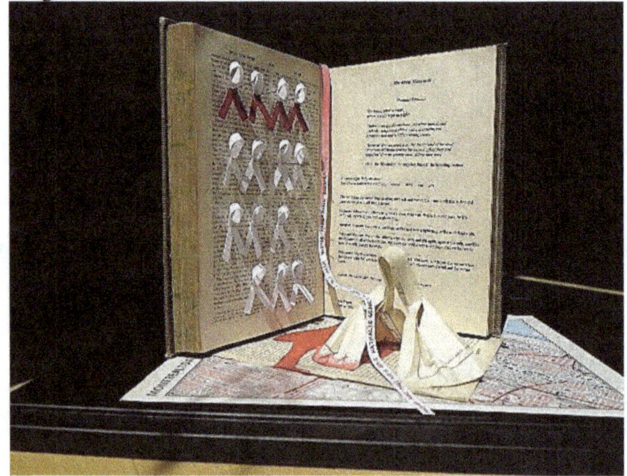

Montreal Massacre, Book Art by Mia Burrus

Runaway Train Nov 2020
Gwynn Scheltema

A runaway train hurtles south
to the end of the world

Once it wound slowly
through great plains and mountains
fuelled by adventure and promise—

now its churning wheels run hot
faster and faster
past the hungry and the homeless
the sick and the dying
the forgotten and the cast-out

It barrels on unstoppable
because it did not take the time
to stop at those places
where it might have gathered strength
been fuelled and fine-tuned
to run without screeching
without smoke and flying grit

Those that ride first class
pull the shades against any new light
intruding upon their card games
hold fast to their toppling piles of chips
round every bend
through black tunnels
seeing nothing but reflections
in mirror glass

Track weary the second-class coaches have fallen
into disrepair, indistinguishable
from third class
couplings grow weaker

with every tenuous mile
soon the last link will break

and the few coaches left will race on
occupants oblivious
content in plush seats
behind velvet drapes

Broken carriages already pile upon the tracks
and when there are no more
clear lines
the train will derail
arc skyward in fire and smoke
hissing and screeching
twisted metal and flying glass

and from the debris
a small clear voice will call to rebuild—
a different train—
a small clear voice will say
"Yes we can!"

West of Hoard Station, Ted Amsden Photography
©2021

Waitressing at Marie Dressler Restaurant
Linda Hutsell-Manning

One of the things Covid has done is to foster nostalgia not only for a return to normalcy but also highlights from days gone by. My 1950's summer waitressing job at Marie Dressler House Restaurant is one of these.

This coveted summer job paid $15 for a six-day week: 11AM to 9PM with two hours off each afternoon. Given I usually made $60 a week in tips, Google says my weekly $75 would be $750 today.

The restaurant owner, Lenah Fisher's high standards for waitresses included speech, posture and attitude. The restaurant sported white linen table cloths and napkins, elegant antique furniture, table settings and silverware. Delighted I made the grade, I knew how gruelling the job would be, having worked two previous summers waitressing at a respected Cobourg hotel.

I rode my bicycle from home on Brook Road South to and from work, rain or shine although, if it was raining, I covered my uniform with a plastic drycleaner bag and carried it on one arm, praying none of it would get water or mud-stained on the way.

Each waitress was designated a room. The Music Room with its antique wind-up music box, belonged to the head waitress whom we all resented. As Maitre D', we felt she took the best customers. On her day off, when Lenah was Maitre D', customer distribution seemed more democratic. Second best was the Button Room—its walls adorned with an extensive collection of glass-framed buttons and, lastly, the Little Back Room which none of us wanted.

We were allotted one cotton uniform: a black below-the-knee dress, a white, tied-at-the-waist apron, a black and white headpiece that required starching and black stockings held up with our garter belt or girdle. We provided black shoes. If the apron became soiled over lunch hour as it often did, I cycled home to wash, hand dry and iron it for the evening shift. We wore these uniforms, according to Lenah, to emulate demure and efficient French maids.

The two-way windowless swinging kitchen door was a nightmare, and I remember disasters with loaded trays. We moved as quickly as possible, always trying to give good service in the shortest time. The rule to be quiet and unobtrusive was certainly broken when two waitresses collided resulting in spoiled orders and an infuriated cook.

One of my compatriots who worked the breakfast shift says Lenah insisted waitresses make and butter their own toast, time-consuming and nerve-wracking when a bus load of tourists arrived. I remember making individual salads and desserts and being told to clean up afterward or face the wrath of the cook Marius.

Ah, Marius! According to Lenah, he was from some posh Riviera restaurant in France. Why he was in small-town Cobourg in the 1950's was, of course, something we were not allowed to question. He ruled with despotic ferocity, often belittling and admonishing us in his Maurice Chevalier accent. The job description said our weekly pay included suppers but Marius was loath to give any of us his French fare. He insisted we wait, even when there was a lull, saying he couldn't give away his prized creations. Paying guests could arrive at any moment. The result was, of course, we stole—a piece of chicken, a slice of beef. We were hungry, having not eaten since breakfast. When he noticed and accused us, we played dumb. "I know I had *dix* pieces of 'cheeckin,' he would sputter, "and now there are only *neuf.*"

We complained and griped but the paycheck plus tips made it worthwhile. Memories have kept the experience alive for me and, I'm sure, for others who worked there in the 1950's.

**Marie Dressler Restaurant Interior, from the
Marie Dressler Foundation Collection**

Harvest Time
Ronald Mackay

Today, as the skin of the cooked beetroot slipped off easily under the gentle pressure of my fingers, I am taken back to the moment my hands first performed that satisfying act. I was four and three hours earlier, had helped my mother lift the raw beetroot from my grandmother's garden.

Back then, responding to a request for help, always resulted in enlightenment and delight.

"Just press slightly and push, Ronald." I do as she bids. The lackluster skin sloughs off to reveal the glossy globe inside, leave my fingers pink and release the warm odour of the earth that nourished it.

Instinctively, my heart swells as this tiny miracle unfolds.

That spring, we'd dug and watched earthworms grow and diminish as they sought escape.

"If the spade cuts them in half, they mend and grow into two worms." Comforting words.

We'd broken clods, raked the bed, opened a drill and planted the seeds separately. We'd watched them poke through and grow. We'd thinned so that the distance between plants was the desired diameter of the beetroot. Later, we'd 'lifted'. We always 'lifted' turnips and potatoes, parsnips and beets. Corn was 'harvested' and 'corn' for us meant barley, oats, and wheat. Berries we 'picked'.

Yesterday, as the skin of the cooled, cooked beetroot slipped off easily under the gentle pressure of my fingers, it surprised me how few of the skills I use these days ever made it onto my *curriculum vitae* so necessary for so many years for an interview or a respectful introduction at a conference.

Now well retired, so much of what I do and COVID encourages, is concentrated into smaller spaces. Much of what is now most valuable, I learned before I went to school, or university, or took professional development to 'keep current'.

Enjoy the song of the morning birds, pick the first rhubarb so carefully as to separate the stalk from the sheath, prepare and plant a garden, thin a row of pale lettuce, lift new potatoes; drop in on an elderly neighbour, call an old friend in a timely fashion before loneliness can set in; send an unexpected greeting; share spontaneous baking with her for whom the gesture is a gift; offer a helping hand.

Today — and the thought surprises me — my 'short bio' might honestly read: *"The most important things in life, Ronald learned from his mother before starting school at the age of five."*

**Ronald sloughing the skins off cooked beetroot,
Photo by Viviana Galleno Zolfi**

Wind Sniffing
Linda Hutsell-Manning

we were to say the least a
motley crew of women
middle-aged recruitments
from the local temp employment
meeting every morning out
behind the plant down in the
parking lot where Joe who
had seen better days waited
in his rusted eighties Ford

he had that lazy I don't give
a damn demeanor as he shifted
from his cigarette and coffee
front seat stance into the chilly
morning air his open shirt
and leather jacket swagger
tough guy stud act just to let us
know what we'd been missing
what we'd never know

we came in cars on bicycles
each weekday usually at ten
dependent on the wind direction
east or south east Joe said
was the best   each here to fill some
economic need   we lined up in
our baggy coats and hats if it was
cold beside his battered car

one by one we took our three
fold sniffs   unscrewed each
cap breathed in the acrid
contents subtle sub text
differences we were expected

to identify and name   then
armed with clipboard map
a daily log   sent off to
stand and sniff and wait

the three suspected gases
unpronounceable   we soon renamed
labeled from our household expertise
Stale Running Shoe was easiest
Fried Rubber stronger   vaguely
reminiscent of some drag race
pop-a-wheelies on hot afternoons
but hard to tell from *Plastic Melt*
especially on the north east side

the plant a great white hulk with
three tall stacks that intermittently
belched out the residue of progress
nestled by the lake   downwind from
school and subdivision   our sniffing
data gathered as a scientific study
labeled neither pro nor con

we walked through fields where
milkweed silk touched goldenrod
past sub divisions   gravel roads
*locate the spot   stand timing for ten
minutes   each two minutes sniff*
our guide a five-point Lichart scale
from *least* to *most*   olfactory glands
tuned up   nose hair antennae on alert

we sniffed   in sun in rain for our next
pay   felt our collective story grow
one woman ordered off the road at
gun point by old Jameson his house
his life now boarded up with anger
and confusion *you git off a here   I
own this land got papers from King
George* Joe laughed   we detoured

came the back way round

one leaf crunch morning sharp with
frost we watched two startled deer
make u turns   slender white flags up
bounding from a meadow formerly
their own and cattle mottled noses
snuffling each green blade
food chain innocents devouring grass
while we marked S or was it H
two at three minutes gagging *five* at ten

day twelve   a foray to the Pentecostal
Camp along the tidy rows of shuttered
cottages and trailers resting from
the summer's daily fervor and conversion
standing sun warm as the scientific minutes
drifted through the leaf dry afternoon
a trinity of entries all absolved and pure

that daily trek back to the parking lot
role switching to our other lives the
camaraderie accumulated stored in
footsteps passing comments rain
wet faces tracking minutes in the wind
that still faint image of us all lined up
across an open field one after one
a silent row of *wise old hags* like
bloodhounds sniffing in the wind

**Sunflower Turning Its Back, Ted Amsden
Photography ©2021**

The Storyteller and the Word
Shane Joseph

In the beginning was the Word, and it was given to the Storyteller, and he told his audience stories that taught valuable lessons about life. Many wise masters followed the example of the storyteller: Jesus, Muhammad, and Gautama, and less exalted ones like Plato, Gandhi, and King.

In the early days, storytellers sat around campfires or stood on mounts to cast their spoken stories to audiences. Hungry listeners lapped them up, for stories were soul food, even said to be messages from God. The Storyteller was in command of his story and his audience, and nothing came between the two except the spellbound air. There was respect for the wisdom imparted and gratitude for the listening. A fair exchange.

Then it was suggested that if these stories were written down, they could be preserved for posterity. The Storyteller complied, and was thereafter called a Writer. By the time we arrived at Marlow, Tolstoy, and Grimm, the printing presses had begun to disseminate stories widely. And there was money to be made in them thar' stories now! Money attracts intermediaries and gate keepers, and they started showing up: publishers, printers, and book shops for starters. Soon, more intermediaries followed: agents, publicists, distributors, editors, proofreaders, writers' associations, advertisers, marketing consultants, literary prize committees. When the internet took hold, even *more* players were added to the mix: website designers, book review mills, e-zines, e-books, blogs, podcasters, video promoters, content aggregators, endorsers, social media. Little by little, the Storyteller was being distanced from his audience. Soon he was only responding to his handlers who told him *what* to write, not what he *wanted* to write.

Then a strange thing happened. The land rose up against the damage wrought by mankind's greed and struck back. The land was fed up with "growth for growth's sake." It released a bug which mushroomed into a pandemic, forcing everyone to hunker in their bunker. To keep the economic engine humming, mankind looked around frantically, and technology came to the rescue, unveiling tools that had hitherto played only among enthusiasts, hobbyists, and bleeding-edge futurists: online shopping went mainstream, "work from home" became the de-facto employment standard, hugging and kissing turned into virtual "likes," and everyone started zooming more and grooming less.

The Storyteller saw an opportunity to claim back what she had lost. She began using the very technology that had earlier dis-intermediated her. She became her own publisher and created a blog to archive and spread her stories for those who still cared to read. She recorded her voice on her smart phone and podcast snippets of her wisdom to millions. She started zooming direct with her audiences, and using social media (the new Hollywood), she streamed video recordings of her stories to more of those unseen millions. She was now directly connected with her audience again, in word, voice, and video, and it was more comfortable than freezing around a campfire or standing on top of a windy mountain. And like in the old days, money did not come into the equation anymore, only the message mattered. The intermediaries didn't matter anymore either. The Storyteller was finally free.

So, in the end, there was the Word, and it remained with the Storyteller.

The Girl from the Attic
Marie Prins

(An excerpt from *The Girl from the Attic*, published by Common Deer Press in 2020. Reprinted with permission of the publisher)

Maddy lives in two worlds. Here Maddy has stepped through a portal to the past into an attic where she peers through a grate to the kitchen below.

Maddy leaned away from the grate, afraid she had been seen by the strangers below her. What were they doing in her kitchen? And why did it look so different? When she peered again through the opening, she saw the old woman wave her hand towards the back door where a rusty squeaking of metal against metal could be heard outside.

"I hear them washing up at the pump, Helen."

"Then sit yourself down, Aunt Ella, and I'll finish the serving." The young woman adjusted a white apron over her long gray and white striped skirt. Why were they wearing those clothes in the summer? They looked awfully hot.

As Aunt Ella plumped a pillow in a chair by the table, boots stomped across the wooden floor. Maddy's nose touched the grate as she bent closer to see the new arrivals. A long-legged boy and a heavy-set man with dark cropped hair entered the kitchen, scraped their chairs over the wooden floor, and settled down at the table below her.

"Where's Eva?" asked Aunt Ella, a note of concern in her voice.

"In the hen house," the boy said. "One of the new chicks is looking sickly. She's fixing a box for it."

"Oh, Clare, shouldn't you be giving her a hand?"

Clare rose in his chair, but before he could stand, a tall, thin girl with brown curls framing a flushed face burst through the door. She held a wooden box. Straw poked over its edges. From inside came a weak *peep-peep.*

"This chick needs a warm place!" Eva pushed the box next to the cook stove's metal legs. She straightened and wiped her hands on her skirt.

A dark shape slunk from under the table and disappeared behind the stove.

"The cat'll get it!" said Aunt Ella.

With a serene smile, Eva shook her head and sat down next to Clare.

"Shadow's just curious." On cue, the black cat with the white tip on its tail sniffed the box and retreated back under Aunt Ella's chair. Eva laughed and picked up her fork.

"To be safe, Clare says he'll put a lid on the box. And he'll feed the chick for me and change its water after I leave. I named it Speckles. After the marks on its feathers."

"Best not get a liking for it," said the older man. "You won't be wanting to eat a chicken that you've named."

"Oh, Uncle Ray, we're not going to eat it! It's a laying hen."

Clare shifted in his chair. "That little peeper may be a rooster, Eva."

Eva took a bite of carrot and chewed it slowly. "Perhaps," she said softly. "But still, it deserves to live." Aunt Ella regarded Eva with sad eyes but said nothing.

Clare stared at his plate. For a few minutes no one spoke. Then Eva covered her mouth and coughed into her hand, a short, tight cough. She put down her fork.

"I'm not hungry," she said. "I think I'll rest till it's time for the train."

Clare jumped up and pulled the rocking chair away from the wall. When Eva sat down, she began to cough again. Reaching into her skirt pocket, she pulled out a large handkerchief and buried her face in it. A long spasm racked her body. When it stopped, a large red stain spread across the white cloth she held in her hands.

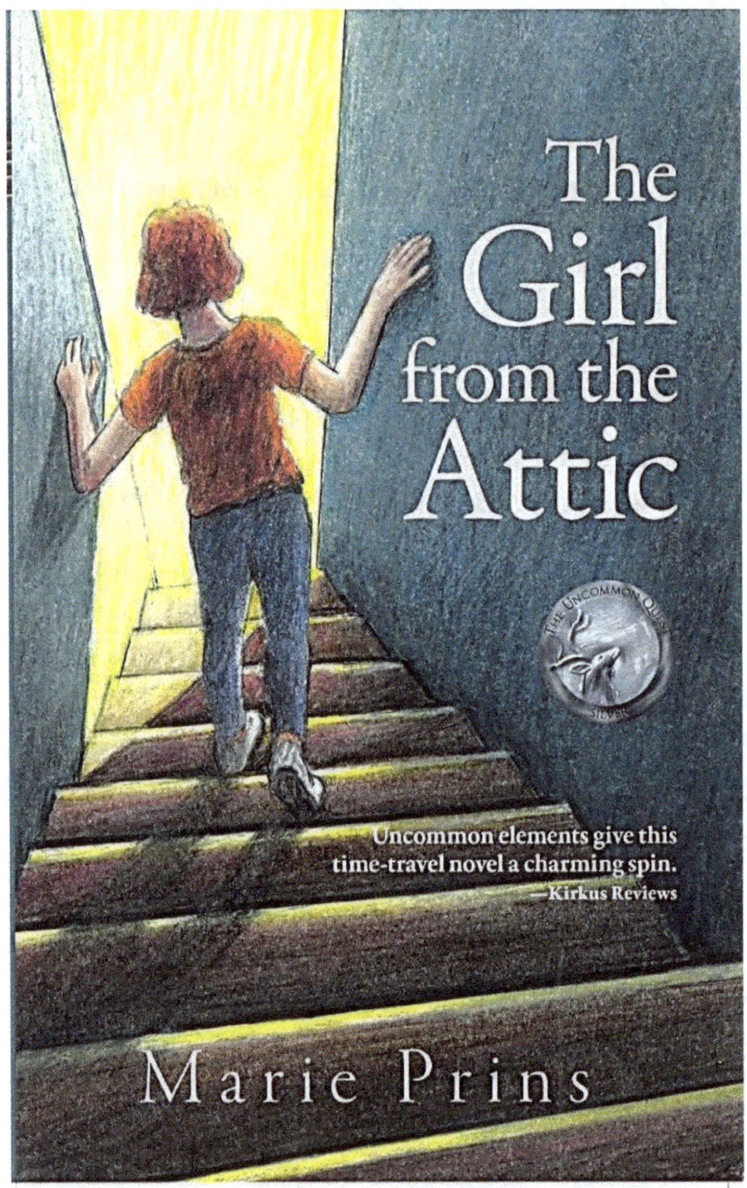

**The Girl from the Attic, Cover Illustration by
Edward Hagedorn**

Nickel
Antony Di Nardo

First time for the moon, first time for the sun,
      first time for the both of us, Nickel and me,
him in his field
         galloping over to the cedar rail,
ears tipped to greet and touch my hand,
            feel my breath,
the trees letting out that one syllable sigh
         they master
in the space of a lifetime.

For one brief moment – it's electric – I sense
         the universe collapsing
    into all we have between us.

That four-year old paint knows everything I do,
    that he needs to know,
        but I have what he wants
and I write it down for him in apples
        and its alphabet.
    I use up an entire store of syllables
to say my name and who I am and where I'm from,
but it's my breath, and nothing more,
        that Nickel needs to read.

Nickel, by Ann Di Nardo

Homesickness
Felicity Sidnell Reid

A ragged bird is swallowed by dark trees
and stirring water, grey as packs of rats,
runs widdershins, below the heavy cloud.
Marge, swaying on the dock, drops to her knees.

Her long dark hair trails down to touch the boat,
but cargo handed over, up she jumps,
her tanned face cracking with both smiles and nerves.
she hauls at jeans and buttons her red coat.

Neighbours drift in close, shouting their goodbyes.
She waves and calls, "I hope we'll be back soon."
Rolling down the long road to Ohio, Frank
will murmur soothing phrases, while she eyes

the crushing weight of concrete towers which swing
across truck windows, like heavy pendulums.
"We will come back," he'll say. "No problem babe!"
But when? Suppressing tears makes sad eyes sting.

Her freedom lost she's curled against the seat,
she has no explanation for the annual dread
she feels as links to her one sanctuary
stretch and stretch—threads so thin must surely break.

The cabin stands on rock strewn shore—at edge
of forest, river, lake and tiny town,
where her family, left behind, still lives.
She chose to leave them, giving Frank her pledge

to make a life with him—and he's the best!
They have work and steady pay in Cleveland,
but she, a compass, always pointing north,
yearns to return—and with the geese to nest.

Autumn Lake, Photo by Gwynn Scheltema

In The Cosmic Wind
Ted Amsden

This morning,
    this bluebell,
        this bee-happy,
            this roadkill-dropped-into-the-organic
                -bin day,

           separating my trash
           facing the risen sun

    in point of shoe

          croc bound,

    in point of mind

          held to waste-separation
                tasks,

    I feel okay.

The pandemic does not roam freely inside the county fence.

My pyramidal cedars crest the roofline.
Soon they will appear in a search engine,
the Cedars of Lebanon faint comparison.
(May Beirut's wounded and hurt curl their fists and thrust
                them
into the face of government incompetence!)
Yes,
    this summer day
        short shorn although hair not so much,
        I trim the blue sail of morning,
        find a keen line into the wind,
        and shout:

Hello Mike One!
Hello Mike Two!

Hello David!
Hello Eric!

All men in the old school sense.
All friends.

Now together.
Funeral images held by a single paper clip.

Hello Mike Wallace!
Hello Mike Milne!
Hello David Medland!
Hello Eric Winter!

What say you now, Boys?
Essence of self reborn or still in staging?
Are you really really dead?

This is the roll call of dearly departed
I shout into the silence of my isolation.

Hello Boys!
Maybe I should turn y'all into fridge magnets!

Mike One (the photographer) says, "Use studio portraits."
Mike Two (the reprobate) laughs like a nasty cherub.
David (first bestie) shakes his head. He never knew me
                                              creatively.
As for Eric, (the poet) irony becomes him best. Ever with a
                                              smirk.

I shout to tell them I am breathing,
have tasks before me, feel a need to push back.

The world too hot,
                too crowded,
                too polluted.

"Have a big crap!" I shout at FlockaOne
the bird formerly known as Blue Jay.

"Shit yacht owners, consumer junkies, resource stealers,
climate deniers, colonialists, into one big steaming pile.
Encourage angry socialists,
                        happy face progressives,
                                green shouting vegans,
                                        - dung beetles all
to roll up our resources and recycle them for humanity."

But that's just an aside.
Covid's got my tongue.
I will not repent.

You hear me Boys?
Just raising the morning flag.
Soon enough the cosmic wind will carry me onward.

                You have a safe day okay?

There is a Message 4 U in Mail Chimp, Richardson Road—Ted Amsden Photography ©2021

Revisiting My Father's Papers and Scrapbooks
Michael Croucher

My father passed in 1974. After his death, his second wife gave me a few boxes containing his personal papers and scrapbooks. I'm so grateful to her for doing that. Those items chronicled parts of my Dad's life that I had little knowledge of. They also helped me to fill in some blanks about my family, and I got to know my dad in a different way. We'd never become really close until the last few years of his life, and of course, I cherished those years.

The process of looking through his papers again during the Covid-19 lockdown, brought back memories of my younger life. One memory inspired this personal narrative. It concerns a sea voyage that brought us a bit closer. I even thought we'd turned a corner. Dad's scrapbook included boarding passes, ship's menus, and other items relevant to the trip. If I ever tire of writing fiction and short stories for long enough to complete a memoir, this narrative will likely be a part of it.

The *Georgic*'s Maiden Departure, Photo from liverpoolships.org

***

Remembering the *Georgic*

I stood beside my dad on the deck of an aging Cunard passenger liner. The *Georgic*. A breeze buffeted my face and hair. The ship's lone stack loomed behind us, its acrid exhaust somehow adding to my excitement. That day and the voyage are still vivid memories. We were leaving to start a new life, and there was the prospect of a new closeness between us.

"She used to have two stacks, Son," he said. "At dinner I'll tell you how she lost the other one. This old girl has quite the history."

It was May of 1953. Along with my mother and an aunt, we were sailing from Southampton to New York. When the voyage ended we'd see whatever we could of Manhattan in the few hours we had before boarding a train to Toronto.

The importance of the trip raised hairs on my neck and made my eyes water. I shivered. Dad reached down and adjusted the collar of my jacket, then placed his hand on my shoulder.

"Once we're underway, we'll go to the cabin and change. You'll put on your new white shirt and the tie before we meet Mom and Aunt Dot in the dining room. I'll tell you all about this ship then."

After our meal he said, "We're crossing to France to pick up more passengers, then it's over to Ireland for another bunch tomorrow. When all the passengers are aboard, we'll sail to Halifax, and then to New York. Quite the adventure for you, Mick."

Mick? Dad never called me Mick. Mostly it was Michael, and only occasionally, the preferred Mike. But Mick was good. The only family member who'd ever called me Mick was my grandad. Dad's dad.

We'd said an emotional goodbye to my grandparents at the Gosport Harbour and took the short ferry ride to Portsmouth. Within an hour of leaving them we were dockside in Southampton and staring up at the ship that would take us away from England. I didn't realize it then, but it would be twenty-four years before I returned. None of us would see Dad's parents again. Crossing the Atlantic back then was not as simple, or relatively affordable as it is now.

Now I get it. I know why Dad called me Mick. That morning when my grandad saw us off, he hugged me, and sobbed out an awkward goodbye. As usual he'd called me Mick. Dad probably knew he wasn't likely to see his parents again. Perhaps he was holding onto every aspect of that moment. That last farewell. He's never called me Mick since. No one has.

Dressed in my new shirt, a God-awful clip-on bowtie—Kelly green with a bright brass crown at the knot—and my new short trousers (English boys that I knew, rarely wore anything but, even in cool weather), and itchy wool socks up to my knees, we met Mom and Aunt Dot in the dining room. Aunt Dot had arrived earlier from London. She'd spent time catching up with Mum while they waited for us to join them.

I hugged Mum and Aunt Dot before taking my seat at the table. Aunt Dot was one of those close family friends who became a *designated aunt*. She looked across at me and winked as Dad took his seat. "Michael, you look very smart today. And I hear you haven't had a *good hiding* yet. That's a good start for any trip."

My Mum chuckled. Dad nodded. He was a good man, a really good man, just a little stiff and standoffish. Like many dads of the time he believed in corporal punishment. His usual threat was to take off his belt and give me a *damned good hiding*. But he never took the belt to me. Ever. He wasn't cruel. He usually conducted his spankings with a folded newspaper. Lots of noise. For me, that was more embarrassing than it was painful.

"He's been a good lad today, Dotty. Holding up very well, all things considered. And he's dressed for the occasion. Suits a tie, don't you think?"

I wondered if one of the *considered* things was that goodbye at Gosport Harbour. My eyes warmed at the mention of it. I fiddled with the bow-tie and kept my head down for a few moments.

Dad's mood was still buoyant. After our prawn appetizer, he looked at all of us in turn. "Imagine this. We're all sailing across the Atlantic. And we're on a rather famous ship. Everybody thought this old girl would never float again, let alone cross an ocean. She served as a troop ship during the war. For a while she was part of the fleet supporting the search for *Bismarck*. The German's bombed her. Left her beached at Port Tewfik, in the Gulf of Suez."

Mum and Aunt Dot didn't bat an eye. They'd likely heard it all before. He was saying this for my benefit. I was all ears. Probably a little bug-eyed. What he'd said fuelled my imagination for the entire voyage.

There was a young Scottish family at the next table. During that first meal, I made friends with a boy my age, Tommy. His family was also going on to Canada. Winnipeg. But they would be leaving the ship in Halifax.

That first night, Tommy and I left the dining room together. As soon as we were out of sight of my parents, I took off the horrid tie. Tommy had called it horrid. "I'd no be wearin' that," he'd said sympathetically. I shoved it in a pocket

Mom called to my back. "Michael, back at the cabin by nine please."

The next morning we were docked in Le Havre. At breakfast Dad's scowl signalled an abrupt turn in his mood. "Where's your tie?"

I responded with a stammer. "I can't find it, Dad. I think I lost it somewhere on the ship." I'd searched everywhere in the cabin for that tie, until I remembered shoving it in the pocket as I left the dining room with Tommy. Somewhere, during that first look-around the ship, the tie must have fallen out.

Dad had left the cabin earlier, eager to pick up a copy of yesterday's late edition of a London paper before breakfast. A limited number of copies had made it across the channel before the ship. Dad's paper snapped open. It hid his face. I knew his scowl was now heavier, and that the paper might soon be whacking my backside. The scowl was set for the day. "Bloody hell," he muttered.

Mom and Aunt Dot stayed quiet through breakfast. Me? I sulked. So much for our fresh start. Dad said he was tempted to confine me to the cabin, except for meal times. Somehow, though, he changed his mind. Maybe Mum and Aunt Dot talked him out of that and my expected *good hiding*. He stayed annoyed at me for much of the trip. That was Dad. I shouldn't have expected anything else.

After the inevitable lecture about responsibility, my excitement about the voyage, the ship, and exploring with Tommy returned. I was out of the cabin within an hour of leaving the breakfast table.

Following our stops in Le Havre and Cork, we began the cold, rough crossing of the Atlantic. Top side was no place to be for most of the trip, so Tommy and I spent hours exploring whatever sections of the ship's interior that weren't off limits, and a few that were. I was fascinated by the still evident damage from the ship's wartime service. Long sections of its passageways were warped and buckled from the bombings and the subsequent fires. Some scars had never been completely covered by her restoration.

We filled the days pretending that we were sailors or troops on the *Georgic* during whatever part she played in the war. Looking back now, if we'd known the full extent of her history, our games could have included the Norwegian coast as well as the Suez for backdrops, or even, with some imagination, the ship's role in the historic chase of the *Bismarck*.

Our war games were interrupted once. We lost a day. Tommy was seasick. Most of the people on the ship—including many crew members—were stricken. I wasn't sick to my stomach, but was quite happy to stay in the cabin that day.

The crossing seemed to go in a flash. I bade Tommy a sad goodbye before his family disembarked in Halifax. My missing tie had shown up, and Dad retrieved it from the purser's office. I was made to wear it for our arrival at New York, so Lady Liberty got to see me at my best. Dad was pumped about seeing Liberty, and anything else we could of the famous city. I'm sure now that he'd purposely booked our passage through New York, even though we only spent a few hours there before catching an overnight train to Toronto.

***

Georgic was a main *character* in the story of our Atlantic crossing. Here's a synopsis of her fascinating history.

She was the last ship to be built for the White Star Line and was launched on November 12, 1931. On January 11, 1933, along with her sister ship *Britannic* she began to sail the Southampton to New York route. On May 10, 1934, *Georgic* became part of the fleet of the newly amalgamated Cunard-White Star Line and worked the London, Southampton, New York passage.

At the beginning of April, 1940, *Georgic* sailed to the Clyde, and work began to convert her into a troopship for 3,000 men. In May the ship assisted in the evacuation of British troops from Andersfjord and Narvik in Norway, landing them at the Clyde. Soon after, she also assisted in the evacuation of troops from Brest and St. Nazaire. The rest of the year was spent transporting Canadian soldiers and carrying troops to the Middle East.

During May, 1941, *Georgic* arrived at Port Tewfik, in the Gulf of Suez as part of a convoy that had been left almost unprotected during the hunt for the German battleship, *Bismarck*. Whilst awaiting Italian internees, on July 14, the ship was bombed by German aircraft and caught on fire. As fires continued to burn, ammunition exploded, wrecking the stern area, the ship was beached on July 16.

It was not until September 14 that a decision was made to try and salvage her. The hulk was raised and then towed to Port Sudan by the ships *Clan Campbell* and *City of Sydney*. Temporary repairs were carried out, and the ship was made seaworthy. In March, 1942, she was towed to Karachi for further repairs. After further cleaning and repairs at Bombay the *Georgic* sailed for Liverpool on January 20, 1943.

Harland & Wolff rebuilt her as a troopship. After the refit, the tonnage had been reduced to 27,268 tons, and the ship now had only one funnel and one mast. During December 1944, she was placed under Cunard-White Star management, and like her sister *Britannic*, retained the buff and black funnels of White Star Line. During 1945, she carried troops to Italy, the Middle East and India.

On December 25, she arrived at Liverpool with troops from the Far East including General Sir William Slim, commander in charge of South East Asia. In July 1948, she arrived at Tyneside for refitting by Palmers Hebburn. The ship was to be used for the Australian and New Zealand emigrant service. In January 1949, she made her first voyage on a route calling at Liverpool, Suez, Fremantle, Melbourne and Sydney.

By May 1950, the ship had returned to the Liverpool-to-New York service for Cunard. During the summer of 1951, the ship sailed on the Southampton-to-New York route. This continued until October 19, 1954, when the *Georgic* made her last voyage for Cunard.

She was scrapped in 1956, three years after my young Scottish friend and I pretended to torpedo U-boats and fight off enemy planes.

Scrapping. What a sad, but predictable end to a wonderful old ship. A ship, that after ten short days became a footnote in my own history.

One of my sons-in-law, a Canadian Naval Officer, did some digging for photos of the *Georgic*. He found some beauties, including one of the ship, crippled after the bombing.

Georgic after the bombing, Photo from liverpoolships.org

Letitia Creighton Youmans 1867

A Brief Biography of Letitia Creighton Youmans: Teacher, Temperance Crusader and Champion of Women's Rights

Allan Seymour

Letitia Creighton was born in 1827 near Baltimore (now Creighton Heights) to John and Annie Creighton.

Letitia began her schooling at age four in a log house, and by age six travelled a mile and a half to Hulls Corners for classes. At sixteen, she boarded at the Cobourg Ladies Seminary, and later, the Burlington Ladies Academy in Hamilton. Two years after graduating, Letitia accepted a teaching position at the Picton Ladies Academy.

It was there that she met and married widower Arthur Youmans.

Letitia's commitment to temperance and battling the evils of alcohol abuse grew through her involvement in her local Methodist church.

In 1874 she travelled to Chautauqua, New York, for a meeting of Christian educators. The Woman's Christian Temperance Union had been founded in the United States that year and temperance meetings were conducted as part of the conference. Youmans returned to Upper Canada inspired, founding the second WCTU Canadian branch in Picton.

The Picton WCTU succeeded in convincing Prince Edward County in 1875 to ban sales of alcohol.

In October 1875 she spoke to a large crowd in Port Hope's YMCA Hall, a rousing return "home" for a now popular speaker. Her message softened to that of "home protection" for women and children.

Letitia's campaigning in subsequent years led her across Canada, parts of the US, and the UK. A normally quiet person, she became Canada's foremost temperance crusader, a fiery orator on stage.

In 1881 Letitia was invited to the White House to meet President Rutherford Hayes and First Lady Lucy Hayes.

In 1883 she met Prime Minister Sir John A. Macdonald—failing to persuade him to ban alcohol. No kidding!

In 1888, with Letitia as President of the Dominion WCTU, the members endorsed women's suffrage. The WCTU was now the largest and most influential women's group in Canada.

Letitia died July 16, 1896, in Toronto. She is buried in Picton.

Her legacy is as a champion for the betterment of women and children in Canada.

Nellie McClung was inspired by Letitia's work, joining the WCTU in 1890. The seed for women's votes had indeed been planted.

WCTU Parade Toronto, Photo from Toronto Archives

The Greatest Fool in the World
Christopher Cameron

When I was writing my memoir, I pinned a review of a friend's book to my bulletin board: "Smart, witty, crafty, informative, nostalgic, yet never pompous, never academic, never self-indulgent…"

Each time I finished a writing session, a page, a sentence, I asked myself, is mine any of these? Can it be?

Writing in English is like building a house with no nails; our words are not fastened together with complicated verb conjunctions or noun cases. The writer has to assemble them so that each one dovetails into another and the result cannot be pulled apart. I set the bar above my reach, as beginners do. I wanted to write clearly but lyrically; to put thoughts in order logically but fantastically; to communicate symbolically but be believed viscerally; to find new ways of saying things that have been said a million million times. To try—like countless others before me—to build that bridge that connects the prose with the passion. To tell stories with words, and have other people read those words.

As a first-time memoirist I gathered lore of writing—good, bad, and useless—around me like piles of sand on a beach. Journalist Denise Balkissoon once remarked that nowadays you can't throw a cat at a pile of books without hitting half a dozen memoirs, most of them about very little of importance. I knew I was adding one more to the pile (thereby increasing the size of the target), but I hoped my memoir would be different. Not important necessarily, just different; something worth throwing a cat at.

I was told often that writing a memoir is like being naked before strangers, but this is a pale and lame metaphor. Naked we all resemble one another, more or less. I wanted to create something that was refreshing and surprising. Are there really that many surprises in smooth, monochrome nakedness? I wanted my writing to reveal more about me than all of my ordinary skin ever could. In my body I am dull and silent; I wanted my words to sparkle and sing.

Virginia Woolf said that a writer vacillates between thinking he is the divinest genius or the greatest fool in the world. I swung back and forth between these states so often that they blended into the same thing. My manuscript became a cat shut in a box, with multiple simultaneous realities. No one will read it. Everyone will read it. No one cares. But they should! Is it as bad/good/thrilling/boring as I think it is? Yes, it is.

Revision 1

At a literary event, I mentioned to a revered memoirist that I had just finished writing my own memoir. Good, he said. Now you have a place to start from. No, I thought, I'm *finished*.

I wasn't.

There began a six-month period of rewriting and revising. I had enjoyed the writing process, but I loved the revisions even more: to have the power to take a sentence written by me, and bend it, patch it, caress it, nail it to another or crowbar it apart. I regularly experienced the morning-after feeling of waking up and looking over at something I had written the night before and wondering how I could ever have thought it was in any way beautiful

I have a tendency to overwrite, so I tacked another quote to my bulletin board, courtesy of novelist Muriel Spark:

"Mrs. Hawkins, I always take great pains with my prose."
He did indeed. The pains showed.

Some writers I know send drafts of their manuscript to everyone from their ex-spouse to the neighbourhood handyman. Some gather their neighbours to sit and listen while they read aloud from the book. I hope they provide refreshments. Wagner used to do this to his friends to introduce his operas; it must have been tedious enough for his audiences, and none of my colleagues is Wagner.

I too entered what I thought was a mandatory period of distributing early drafts to amateur readers for their opinion. Some I asked, but more asked me: oh please! I would love to read your book. So in my greenness I sent my raw, unpolished words to twelve people. I don't know what I was expecting—I heard back from exactly four people, two of whom actually got to the end. Excuses drifted in like so much flotsam. One woman wrote to me saying that her reading of my manuscript was going slowly because she was between laptops and was having trouble seeing it on her iPhone. I became sure the rest of them were avoiding me, embarrassed to face me with either their withering critiques or the fact that they had never gotten around to reading it. I never heard again from at least two of them. None of this boded well for sales if my book ever got into the market.

When I thought the book was finished, I decided I wanted someone to publish it. I didn't care if I ever made a penny from sales, I just wanted verifiable evidence that someone else had read my story and had liked it enough to print it at their expense. Query letters went off, informing the recipients how witty, fascinating, and informative my book was. I told the small presses that I wanted the intimacy of a small press. I told the big Toronto publishers that I wanted the power and reach of a big Toronto publisher. I described my ideal reader for them. I told them what an interesting guy I was. I outlined how I would market the book, how accessible it was, how successful it would be. Then I waited to hear from them as a Victorian spinster would wait for a gentleman caller.

While I was writing, I earned a certificate in publishing and became an editor, hoping to learn something about the business. What I learned was that most likely no one would ever look closely at my manuscript as it lay in the slush pile. (I pictured real slush, my words melting and flowing in inky rivulets down a pulpy, forgotten mountain of over-the-transom paper.) Or at best, an intern a third my age, who was still attempting to fully grasp the correct uses of the apostrophe, would read a few pages, scanning for a marketable hook. I tried to network (there is a whole chapter in my memoir devoted to what a lousy networker I am). I had some tenuous connections and I used them shamelessly, buying lunches and beer for people I would never spend ten minutes with under other circumstances.

But I was mostly rearranging deckchairs. Eventually I got out of the habit of checking my email at the end of every day to see if a publisher or agent had responded to my query. Of looking in the Trash folder in case their reply had gone there by mistake. Of thinking, at 5:00 PM: Well, they're two hours behind in Calgary; there's still time to hear from the people out there.

It is a vigil I would not wish on any writer. I think that Charles Bukowski was right about the whole writing thing. Unless you have a sun inside you burning your gut forcing you to do it…you probably shouldn't.

Revision 2

There were temporary flashes of hope, like those times when someone you are unrequitedly in love with speaks to you, private and vulnerable, and briefly you want nothing evermore from life; and then the next day she looks through you with blank eyes. An excerpt from the manuscript was published in a music magazine. I read one of the stories on CBC, and a chapter at a pub storytelling event. One publisher asked to see more—then sent a polite rejection several months later. After extensive, shameless research, I reconnected with a woman who has a featured role in the memoir. I had been besotted with her in high school. She liked the story I'd written about her, and for a brief moment I was besotted all over again.

One of the rejections I received contained some thoughtful and useful advice: we think you are trying to do too much with your book, they said, and this is blurring the focus. Concentrate on one voice, tone, and theme. I started another round of revisions; this time I was a refiner's fire. I interrogated each word as if it were a potential saboteur. There was no neutral ground: a sentence was either for me or against me. Anything I decided didn't contribute to the cause was liquidated.

I began again—again and again. My book was beginning to feel like the Ship of Theseus, containing almost none of the parts it had set out with. I questioned myself and my motives daily. I wondered whether I was even still writing about myself, or about some new character born from the sea foam of the memoir. I began to think about my lead character as I would a fictional one, as if he were someone I was meeting for the first time instead of someone I had lived with all my life. His body and what he did with it, his surprises, confusions, triumphs, and disasters were now appearing new to me. Could I even recognize my life story anymore? A colleague once reminded me that our characters have the power to achieve a type of grace that is not given to us as their creators. Who, exactly, had I created?

Well, it was me, of course. But a new me that had not existed before I had written about him. I had filled in an outline of my life using nothing but words.

So now I had a clear, well-crafted manuscript that still didn't seem worth reading.

Revision 3

This is where the arc of my memoir-writing storyline touches the earth. An author's truism says that you should write the kind of book you would like to read. Eventually I decided that if it wasn't going to be published anyway, I would write the book I wanted to *write*—without any outside input or agenda except to finish it.

One school of memoir writing tells us that we have to open up painful old memories, like jars of outdated preserves, and spread them out for the world to examine; that the pain we relive in our writing is an important ingredient in a successful memoir. This is a well-worn path successfully trodden by many authors, but it wasn't going to work for my story. The part of my life I was writing about had been fun and fulfilling. I couldn't make it otherwise.

I took out swaths of text I had put in for reasons I never understood. The existential angst and artistic crises I had contrived were excised, bottled in formaldehyde, and saved for transplant into some future book—one that requires angst and crises.

In her book, *Still Writing*, Dani Shapiro quotes Martha Graham in a letter to Agnes DeMille: "It is not your business to determine how good it is; nor how valuable it is; nor how it compares with other expressions. It is your business to keep it yours, clearly and directly..."

And so it became mine. This was where I arrived after my final round of revisions: not to judge, not to measure, but just to own what I was writing. In this way my story's voice was born.

One of my goals had been to fill in the outlines of characters and settings that were fading into shadows in my memory. Within the parameters of truth I had set out for myself, I kneaded and shaped my tales—my theme, tone, and voice—until I believed I had something that was truly readable. Entertaining, even.

I decided to send out some last Hail Mary queries to publishers I had not thought of the first time around. At the end of one month I had received two rejections and—from a small literary press—one request for the complete manuscript. A few weeks later the small press wrote to say that they had loved my book, thought it was beautifully written, and wanted to publish it. A contract arrived, looking just like the samples I had studied in my publishing course. It promised an advance that I was sure would never be covered by any sales. Even after the contract was signed I couldn't believe that it would actually happen. I was still waiting for someone to tell me they had made a mistake; that it wasn't my book they wanted after all; that they had sent the offer to the wrong person. I was prepared for my literary career to be like Stephen Leacock's financial career, begun and ended in a few farcical moments.

Nonetheless, one beautiful spring day, the 85,000 words I had thought up about my life and assembled one at a time became a book.

So, it was published. How cool is that? There were launches and interviews and readings. I worried that no one would like it, but some did. Enough did.

I wonder what is next. I doubt my memoir will ever be considered a big deal by anyone except me. All I can be is impressed with the whole concept of writing: that I wrote some words and that someone else read them. I don't know that I built any bridges that connect prose with passion. I still consider myself a journeyman writer, a capable wordsmith, with experiences that comprise only the predawn of the day when I can call myself an author. But now I can hold my own book in my hand. Now I can pin my own reviews to my bulletin board.

Now I have a place to start from.

Chris Cameron, Photo by Chris Cameron

WINTER 2020-2021

Even Storm Troopers Get the Blues, Dwellissimo Store Window, Port Hope—Ted Amsden Photography ©2021

Stanchion!
Mia Burrus

for John

and but for the sky there are no fences facing
Bob Dylan

more than a fence to slow the blowing snow
stanchionesque stockades put on a show
of guarding the shifting sands of status quo
impaling the hearts of the fenced
with ignorance made manifest

but for trees there'd be no fences facing
the tree alive teaches you to love the sky
it feeds its own leaves freedom to depart
laden with fruit its bending branch
bows down, earth-grateful, full of grace

but for lifeless fences facing in your mind
you are free to stand (buttress or blockade?)
free to bend and resonate, be lute, sitar,
marimba, flute - your song the limitless
sky - the freedom, unconstrained, to fly

Stanchion by Mia Burrus

What Remains
Cynthia Reyes

The colours have come and gone
You know the ones
Revered in poems and short stories
In blog posts and books
The reds, the golds, the crimsons
Deep pinks and oranges and apricots
Dazzling us with their glamour
Then falling in the cold winds of November
Turning brown and dry on the earth below
So what remains?

What remains is what was there before:
The sturdy trunks of oaks and maples
The birches, beeches, willows
The grey-brown bark their only cover
Rooted in the hillsides of our little valley
Their branches giving rest to birds in flight
The robins in their dozens
The doves in their pairs
The blue jays, in flashes of blue and grey
An avian caravan on its way
The annual trip to somewhere warm
What remains?

A few brave ones remain
The doves and chickadees
The cardinals, their brilliant red
Glowing from the branch of the evergreen spruce
The squirrels, in grey and black
Their fur thick for winter
The memory of salmon
Dozens, hundreds, perhaps thousands
Struggling their way upstream
To spawn.

And the memory that someone saw a bear here once
And heard a coyote howl

What remains?

What remains was ever thus
The iron-grey water of the stream
Gliding surely between its banks
A glint of silver as it rushes over rocks
In a never-ending journey toward the lake
And the first snow on trees and grass
And white on white, un-peopled chairs
Left outside to overwinter
And the knowledge that in this valley
Autumn is always followed by winter
And winter by spring
And if we're lucky, we too shall remain
To see another summer
And another autumn
When the colours return, glorious.

Barbarians at the Gates
Shane Joseph

Once upon a time, a benevolent prime minister looked upon the land and decreed that we would no longer be diminished by books written in the UK and America only, that Canadian writers would stand tall and be recognized for their talents. He opened a war chest to fund fledgling publishers and to assist writers who couldn't make a living solely by their trade. Universities and colleges also came to the fore by seeing an opportunity to spread creative writing courses across the land, provide employment to writers on a more permanent basis, and cash in on the largesse of government grants for literary and educational programs. Can Lit was born.

For the next twenty-five years this effort blossomed, and Canadian writers reached the world stage. We won literary awards locally and internationally. Then something started to go wrong. After that benevolent PM's exit from the stage, subsequent politicians did not see value in the arts as he had. They did not see that a sign of a mature society is the blossoming of its arts, not just its economy; they did not see that the arts industry, when viewed by its broadest definition, was the largest employer in Canada. They did not see that Canada's population had virtually doubled from when the benevolent PM had attained his enlightenment, and that there were many more stories to tell. What these unenlightened politicians saw instead were budget deficits, and the easiest way to address the problem was to cut frivolous funding—to the arts, for instance.

Net result: barriers to entry shot up in Can Lit as funding shrank. It's Marketing 101. If you create scarcity, prices and sales can be protected for those *within* the gates. Replacements to the existing stock of anointed writers would only be made selectively, when older ones retired. And the replacements would be younger ones who were likely to produce another 10 books per author during their lifetime. Net-net result: "barbarians" started gathering outside the Can Lit gates. Who were these barbarians? The excluded ones: older writers, retirees writing the stories they always wanted to write, those who did not luck in with the right book at the right time, those with good stories but poor literary connections. There were writers from ethnic communities, marginalized writers of colour, creed and sexual orientation, memoirists, poets, and other misfits. They all needed a home if the burgeoning creative appetite of this land was to be satiated.

Enter the small presses, those unfunded ones who by dint of personal conviction, limited private funds, grit, and using the internet, carved out an existence. They provided shelter to the barbarians. These unfunded presses do not enjoy lavish award galas or invitations to literary festivals, or reviews in national newspapers; they create their own awards and festivals, with their own funds, within their communities, and rely on personal contacts for reviews and interviews of their work, placed in "virtual" street corners where readers gather. They are vulnerable to the spectre of financial failure; their grasp has to be within their reach, and they cling like leeches to the hides of online distributors such as Amazon, Apple and Kobo. Heavens forbid a health crisis, for these one or two-person shops need all hands on deck to push a book out the door. But like the Energizer Bunny, they keep going, because Can Lit is no longer that inner sanctified layer of chosen ones but also this rougher outer layer that embraces, and feeds the inner circle, and in turn embraces the traditional channel's rejects.

Welcome to the new and improved, and expanded, Can Lit!

Turning Down Social Media's Volume
Michael Croucher

During this pandemic, staying informed is vital to our health, but being obsessed with the news, whether about Covid-19, the gong show that is American politics, politics in general, or a world in chaos—as it has been for generations, and will likely stay in for decades to come—is really damaging to our sense of well-being.

I backed off most of my social media accounts a couple of years ago. Now I've reduced my Facebook time drastically. The issues people gnash their teeth over on Facebook are all critically important, and don't get me wrong, I have strong opinions about them as well, but I will not be adding to the noise level.

I enjoy Facebook. It keeps me in touch with friends, other readers and writers, and with relatives in England. Those abilities alone are a huge plus. I enjoy the interesting articles, photographs and insights that people post, and I try to post the same in return. I've had people ask why I don't express my opinions regarding the news. The answer is simple, even in retirement, and even during the pandemic, mostly shut in, I have a life to live. I don't want to waste time in a *digital schoolyard*, bickering over opinions.

I'll stay informed through limited daily exposure to network news and listening to the occasional podcast, Peter Mansbridge's *The Bridge*, for example. Other than that, my screen time on TV is mostly dedicated to shows I enjoy: *Masterpiece Theatre*, other drama shows, and hopefully, if they can get back to it safely, some hockey games. On my laptop, I'll do research, write, and yes, check in on Facebook. But I won't be making any noise.

Jupiter Rising
Christopher Black

To see Jupiter rising in a May evening sky,
an arcing bright light among shivering leaves
and early white blossoms of an old cherry tree,
caused me to think of my brief passage through time
as the rise and the fall of a lone shooting star,
a wanderer, from nowhere, who's gone in a flash,
while the planet, unchanged, moves still on its path,
and the leaves, from bright green, turn to autumnal gold,
then fall, and decay, yet with spring are reborn,
while the blaze that was me is now just smoke and dark
dust.

Photo by Ann Di Nardo

How to Use a Cow's Horn as a Paintbrush

Ronald Mackay

For reasons more obvious to a teenager than to an octogenarian, our grandchild stopped reading. We gifted him our favourite books. We took him to the bookstore so he might select a book of his choice. But he had stopped reading.

Taking a cue from his love of his iPad, I sought out links to science-based podcasts trying to match the interests he had displayed since he mastered mental arithmetic before he was five. His response suggests compliance rather than enthusiasm. I strive to insinuate myself into that adolescent mind to uncover why.

Tidying my study, I found the framed photograph of my grandmother. Tinted 1940's style, it captures the Nanny who consoled us when we were overwhelmed by shined boots and slung rifles in foreign uniforms marching to Polish orders that needlessly alarmed us.

I search that face, those trust-inspiring eyes that we took for granted, trying to fathom her thoughts at that moment, who they were with, what hopes she had for a future after such war.

I struggled to put myself in the place of a successful physicist but failed parent, trying to capture what impelled him to reject his first-born. To one who has never fathered but who has felt the comfort of a tiny hand in his, to choose never to set eyes on a child made in love, poses a mystery. The result was a play that, partially at least, satisfied director, actors, playwright, and audience.

Encouraged, I now inhabit the mind of Leonhard Euler's last and thirteenth child. Magda is motivated to assist her father to resolve the 18th Century puzzle of the Seven Bridges of Konigsberg. Nightly, I occupy not only her adolescent mind, but that of her gentle mother and her father, famous for reconciling conflicts inherent in Isaac Newton's calculus.

During the Cold War, within the walls of Horezu, a 17th century monastery on the Wallachian Plain, Pearl and I watched a Romanian artisan recreate an ancient and variously coloured ceramic stove. We watched him fabricate new tiles by hand, to match the old. Once dried, he traced the traditional pattern onto the new before their firing.

On his workbench sat a rack of cow horns each filled with a coloured liquid concocted by him. Colours that bore no resemblance to those of the finished tiles. "Firing will provide colour," he told us.

To understand his unlikely choice of brush, I immersed myself in his crouched concentration. He used each cow horn as we first learned to use nibbed pens. Ink, neither too little nor too much. A light touch. Confident strokes following rules of penmanship and artistry.

This is what we writers do. We occupy the minds of those we are not, inserting ourselves into lives we know not. Seeking. This is what we must do.

Blame Me for This Pandemic. It's All My Fault
René Schmidt

Seriously. I may have asked for this awful time. My wife, who understands these things better than I do, says I always get what I ask for. Once again she may be right.

Last year I looked up and saw the sky crisscrossed with a dozen contrails where jets had sucked in clean air and spewed out unburned fuel...*so I wished for a reduction of needless jet travel.*

A week later I parked beside a massive, clean and shiny overpowered pickup truck driven by a tiny woman buying groceries. That truck wasn't bought to haul bricks or pull a drilling rig...*So I wished people wouldn't drive huge vehicles needlessly.*

That night I took my wife to a fast food restaurant where people gorged themselves on deep-fried and sugary foods (and yes I ate some) *and wished we all would eat at home more and learn to cook healthy stuff.*

A teacher friend complained her students didn't appreciate school like the students in Africa she taught years ago...*I found myself wishing school meant so much our kids would want to go.*

So blame me. I got what I wanted, though in a way that says, 'be careful what you wish for.'

There's another thing I am wishing for: *that people won't trust sloppy, speculative, wrong, or hateful nonsense that can often be found on the Internet, nor believe the self-serving tweets of a certain leader of the free world. I hope and pray that wish will come true.*

Years ago I included epidemics, pandemics and various health crises in my Canadian Disaster books. I spent months researching each story using multiple and reliable sources. I learned a lot. Someone asked recently if I was working on a sequel about this Covid-19 pandemic. But honestly, right now I couldn't. How do you get your head around almost 13,000 dead in Canada with the number still rising? How can you explain anti-mask protesters shouting in the streets or the anti-vaccine movement knitting plots and conspiracies about doctors trying to harm us? (And for the record, similar movements happened during our previous health crises, but I can't explain that thinking.)

What I know is, except for some remote communities in the North, we in most of Canada have had an unprecedented 60-year stretch of robust healthiness compared to other countries. Thank God for vaccines, antibiotics and free health care! Thank God for Canadian governments, with all their flaws and failures, for supporting a pretty good health care system. It's not perfect, but it's a whole lot better than what it could be without dedicated leaders. These people have the nerve to tell us to stay at home and keep away from crowds and isolate and to celebrate Christmas in small numbers. And I'm glad they have the courage to tell us, because friends, this isn't over yet.

School's out for the Holidays
Felicity Sidnell Reid

Afternoon darkness cloaks
the road. The school bus,
late, puffs up the hill.
Its stop signs shoot
out, left and right,
as it stands still.

Scarlet paddles open, glow
on pumpkin coach, not
yellow school bus,
as small dark shadows,
fearing nought, leap
into the piled-up snow.

Towards a string of diamond lights
each cluster marking someone's house,
a band of spirits twirl and dance.
They call like birds in their delight
as lit up firs show them the way
and reindeer on a rooftop prance.

School Bus, Photo © Patricia Calder

Skates Off
Tom Pickering

For the whole month of December twelve-year old Will had been telling his parents he wanted a new pair of skates for Christmas.

Will felt a new pair of skates might help his game. He had a good head for hockey but skating was his downfall. A lot of times, he just couldn't get into the play quickly enough because his wobbly ankles failed him.

In the lead up to Christmas, he maintained a persistent public relations campaign. Over dinner table conversation, he would drop a comment here and there. Hey Dad, you know Andy two doors up? Last year, he got a new pair of skates for Christmas and he's become a really good player.

During the last community league hockey game before Christmas, Will turned around for a puck, lost his balance, and fell flat on his face. A few of the other kids laughed at him. He held back tears. Who was he kidding? This wasn't the first time he fell flat like that. He didn't just stumble, he hit the ice like a kid hitting the water in a belly flop—hard, loud, and painful. It was obvious this wasn't his game. He was great at road hockey. He could outrun all the other kids and score goals. Add ice, and he sucked.

He stopped talking about new skates at the dinner table. He wished he hadn't even started the whole stupid campaign. Will vowed to drop hockey next year and take up bowling or ping pong.

Christmas morning came, and Will opened his presents going from smallest to largest. The very last present, wrapped in a large box with a bow, was a new pair of skates. They were sleek, black, shiny, and they were fantastic.

A few days later, he and his parents drove to a nearby outdoor skating rink. Will entered the small, unheated change room to lace up his new skates.

He stepped on to the ice surface and glided around, feeling a little firmer in his new skates, but fighting a slight wobble as he made sweeping turns. He knew in his heart that skating and playing hockey was never going to be his sport.

After a while, they all got cold. It was time to go. Seated in the change room, Will wondered how to fake being enthusiastic about his new skates. Outside, his parents were standing there waiting for him. His dad noticed right away. Where are your skates, he asked.

Will's heart sank. He ran back into the change room. No skates. Had they fallen off the bench? No. Had someone hung them up somewhere? No. It was too much to bear. In a matter of a few moments, they had been stolen. Will, how could you do this, his father screamed. Do you know how much they cost? Will, this is absolutely awful, his mother icily chimed. His parents got him what he wanted, and look what happened. After enduring Will's entreaties for a month, they had every right to be angry.

Will hung his head in shame. They drove home in silence. He went to bed in silence, not saying goodnight to his parents. Nor did they say goodnight to him. Lying in bed, Will dreamed of baseball season. He could run fast. He could catch the ball. He had an arm like a cannon. Best of all, no one stole baseball gloves.

Cobourg West Beach Winter, by Kim Aubrey

Christmas and the Great Coverup
Eric E Wright

I've always loved Christmas. The carols. The Christmas trees. The lights. The manger scenes. Christmas Eve services in a candle-lit church. The whole extended family gathering around a table groaning with turkey and all the fixings. Laughter and old stories. But this is the Covid-19 year and we've got social distancing and masks. No family hugs. No visits from our family in Mississauga. Certainly none from Atlanta. Sigh.

The isolation has given us all more time to think about what is important in our lives. Family is way up there. So are friends, which is one reason we always look forward to Christmas cards and greetings. It has also heightened the importance of basic values; democratic values, moral values of integrity, compassion and, dare I say it, faith in Jesus, the Christmas One. He actually came to re-acquaint us with the Creator and Sustainer of the universe.

This Covid year has also seen the promotion of various causes. We've been reminded of the cruel details of slavery and residential schools. The media have made acts of injustice that represent failures of our vaunted liberal democracies hard to ignore. We must do all we can to ensure they are not repeated.

But here is a strange thing. We seem content to disguise the real cornerstones of western civilization beneath frivolous symbols.

Christmas is a case in point. Instead of heralding far and near the birth of the most astonishing person history has ever seen, we allow Santa Claus and his Elves to smother the celebration. The journey to Bethlehem is forgotten beneath the blaring of Ho, Ho, Ho's, dreams of a white Christmas, and a whole rinky-dink plethora of substitutes. It's Rudolph, the red-nosed reindeer, the Grinch and Frosty, the snowman. Christmas trees, yes; creches, no—too religious.

Christmas is not alone in this drive to hide religious symbols and secularize. There's St. Patrick's Day disguised beneath shamrocks and green beer instead of celebrating an amazing missionary figure who led the transformation of Ireland. Instead of Easter heralding the resurrection, we have Easter eggs and bunnies. Reformation Sunday is completely ignored in spite of the fact that this revolution prepared most of the western world for democracy with its emphasis on the dignity and freedom of the individual. It was the reformation that laid the groundwork for abolishing the divine right of kings and establishing the sovereignty of the individual.

Sour grapes? I am not espousing a series of joyless celebrations. Kids deserve lots of fun, times to dress-up, eat candy and receive presents. But as Santayana has said, "He who fails to learn from history is doomed to repeat it." Sadly, we can see the signs of this failure all around us. The more we disguise or ignore the real sources of our belief in the dignity, moral responsibility and freedom of the individual the more quickly will we see our civilization deteriorate.

Something else to ponder besides masks, hand-washing and social distancing.

Jazz in the Time of Pandemic, or, Sax in the City
Alan F. Bland

When asked to play my sax for an online Christmas Show, I said, "Sure. I just have to work on my "chops." I hadn't played much during the shut-down. I had felt guilty every time I walked past my sax sitting lonely and un-played on its stand.

What to play? Maybe a Thelonious Monk tune, "Round Midnight," a slow blues, but maybe that was a bit too bluesy. Or Paul Desmond's classic "Take Five," more upbeat. Yeah, that was the one. So, to work. If a horn player does not work those "chops" daily, then he or she loses the muscle control around the mouth, the muscles that control what is known as the "embouchure." With a weak embouchure you leak air and blow raspberries; not good. Gradually it came back, and after a week or so of playing longer each day, I had found my sound again.

But back to the instrument. It is a Selma, the Steinway of saxophones. I bought it in Paris, where they are made, in 2001, and had it shipped home. Not just any Selma, this one is finished in black lacquer, and with the brass fittings it is a sight to behold. For what it is worth there are over eight hundred parts to a saxophone, and they all need to be in sync. I had had it serviced recently at Bb Music in Peterborough, and it was playing just fine. It's not just pianos that need tuning.

As an aside, when I came back through Toronto customs and declared the sax that would be arriving later, I was happy to hear that there was no duty to pay, as saxophones are not made in Canada. My paperwork was stamped just as a large fellow at the next table was asked to open the two huge suitcases he had brought from Jamaica. They were filled with bottles of rum. We all watched as every bottle was poured into the sink at the back of the room.

Who says that travel is not enlightening?

No travel these days though. Reality began to set in. Brass and Wind instruments cannot play chords and can only harmonize when there is more than one, or when other instruments are in the mix. Brass and Wind instruments play one note at a time. You can play notes in a chord in sequence but not the way a pianist or guitarist can. So, what would my sax sound like when played back through the speakers on a lap-top? Well, those speakers should be called "squeakers." I decided that, like so many other things, my solo would have to wait.

The Good, the Bad, and the Ugly
Shane Joseph

I review books, and have a few hundred posted in the public domain. Of late, I have resorted to writing reviews only of the books I like and politely turn away many that I don't, author notwithstanding. Why? Because reviews sell books, I'm told. But what I have experienced is that while good reviews do not necessarily sell books, a bad review by a respected reviewer can stop a book in its tracks. And I do not want to hurt anyone's career, unless they are established writers now resorting to writing junk and riding on their fame, and who are in dire need of a wake-up call.

It is important to understand the reviewer's background and agenda before submitting a book for review. We all have limited experiences, and our backgrounds colour our views on the world and how we respond to literature. Different reviewers from different backgrounds and with different levels and types of education may review the same book differently.

Why do we write reviews? Like me, to remember what we have read so we can refer back to our review in conversation? To enter the literary debate and provoke discussion? To make a name for ourselves, particularly in this social media universe where we have to publish frequently in order to stay relevant? To take a power trip and destroy writers that have made it through sheer luck and influence while our own literary ambitions have languished due to a different combination of luck and influence? To have followers and admirers who pick their books based on our comments? For money, even though there isn't much there anymore? To extend the maxim of, "those who cannot do, teach"—thus, "those who cannot create, criticize?" Perhaps it's due to a combination of all the above.

Once a book is in the public domain, a raft of vested interests descend upon it: publicists who gather supporters to write nothing but glowing reviews; sycophantic fans of a popular writer who cannot say anything bad and can quickly flood a Goodreads or Amazon posting with plaudits, making a critical review look out of place; the vengeful reviewer, who says nasty things with no means of backing it up but who serves to create doubt in the minds of neutral readers looking for a good read. Some authors even create alter-ego reviewers to review their books and post the most spellbinding reviews of their own work—it has a neutralizing effect on all those bad reviewers and may place an invisible "cease and desist" order on them.

A book is an argument between a writer and a reader that the latter can never hope to win. And a review is the opposite; the writer cannot win, especially when faced with a negative review. I have often believed that it is better to have one's book read widely than to have it reviewed widely, for the wider you cast the review net, the easier it is to catch one of those reviewer types I have described above. And yet, the current trend is to gather as many reviews as possible because the number of reviews seems to correlate with the number of books sold. And while that wisdom may hold true in some cases, quantity does not always reflect quality.

Despite the cautions listed above, the book review remains a clear example of a reader's total engagement with a book, and if done right, can be a source of encouragement, feedback, and sanction to the author and to other readers.

Shane Reading, Photo by Sarah Jacob

Journal Entry: Friday, January 25, 2002
Peggy Dymond Leavey

For years I have kept a journal, and from time to time, I dip into it. Here is an entry from Friday, January 25, 2002:

I've been listening all morning to tributes on the radio to the late Peter Gzowski. Born in Toronto in 1934, Peter was a journalist and interviewer, the youngest-ever managing editor of *Macleans'* in the 60s, a *Globe and Mail* columnist, and during the 1980s and 90s, the host of a popular morning show on CBC.

I was on my way to work this past Wednesday when I heard the news that Peter was very ill and had been admitted to hospital. Then, last evening, came the news that he had died. He was only 67.

Peter's radio show was part of my life for years, and although I'd lost track of him after he left the CBC, I did hear him again not too long ago, talking to poets Patrick Lane and Lorna Crozier about his contribution to their book on addictions. Peter's radio audience had been aware of the struggle he'd had with emphysema.

As a young wife and stay-at-home mother I used to listen every day to "This Country in the Morning" and to his newest program called "Morningside." But it was those first broadcasts I remember best. I remember Danny Finkleman being a regular, how the two of them would dissolve into fits of laughter so that I could imagine the whole cross-Canada audience breaking up.

My mother was the one who first introduced me to morning radio. She was newly retired from teaching, and she and I would chat on the phone about what we'd just heard on Bruno Gerussi's CBC show. She called him "Bruno," as if they were personal friends. We wondered what the new man taking over the time slot would be like. It didn't take long to discover that he was terrific.

This morning I dug out my Gzowski memorabilia. There's a battered copy of "This Country in the Morning" that I'd requested for Christmas and could hardly put down for weeks afterward. There's a booklet of pickling recipes I sent for, and a copy of "The Morningside Papers." I have as well a cassette tape of Peter's show on the day that Shelagh Rogers read my Christmas story. As a contributor to the story contest I received a copy of Stuart McLean's new book. Stuart had been another regular on the show, and the on-air antics of the pair of them are legendary.

I heard from several people who'd heard my story on the air that December morning—an old friend in New Brunswick, my brother-in-law on his way to work in Ottawa. That was the thing about Peter's show. You knew people all across Canada were listening to that wonderful, smoke-infused voice. It was like all of us were joining hands.

Radio, Photo by Mia Burrus

Winter Song
Jessica Outram

sounds of the next generation
voices and violins and winter child
songs of a thousand beautiful things
amid this safe harbour

underneath stars and lullabies
glorias celebrate our days of beauty
sharing peace on strings
and music to all

Snowy Trees, Photo by Kim Aubrey

Song Tree
Jessica Outram

my song
starts softly
roots and soil

seed chords
sprouting story
toes stretch

melody gliding
crown to clouds
notes

falling as leaves
rising as butterflies
I surrender

knees and elbows
swing and ring
this song heals

shoulders as branches
sounding the depths
of my senses

to realize beauty
standing in one place
every season

The Gifts of 2020
Gwynn Scheltema

If there's one thing that I have learned during 2020, it's the importance of kindness and acceptance and the finding of joy and fulfilment in the unexpected, big and small. And part of that is the acceptance of self, flaws and all. So, in 2021, I've decided I am going to put kindness to myself first in any plans I make or goals I set, and strive for participation and passion, not perfection.

Unexpected writing gifts

Someone once said that if you think your glass is always half empty, then pour it into a smaller glass and quit whining. I tried to take that approach in 2020 whenever new annoyances and problems arose, and realized that out of a seemingly all bad year, a number of things did go well for me.

I live out in the country, a good hour from all the people and events and activities I like to engage with. By May, a general acceptance of Zoom and work-from-home meant I didn't have to spend so much time travelling. That gave me more time for myself and my writing—a true gift.

And technologically, Zoom was just the start. I gained a whole gift bag of new skills: how to make videos, how to convert MP4s created on a phone to edited podcasts. I gave my first on-line workshop, becoming familiar with break-out rooms, gallery views, split screens and converting in-class learning materials to the screen. An arts group I volunteer with went virtual with Google Groups and Google Meet and is planning virtual arts activities I would never have imagined were even possible.

I took part in virtual writing critique group meetings, online workshops and paint nights. I had time to read more. I enjoyed countless free offerings of art of all disciplines from around the world.

So much to fill my creative well and give me new ideas. Another wonderful gift.

Being stuck at home allowed me to work on habits—breaking old bad habits and cultivating new ones to replace them. On the writing front alone, I have been able to get back into journalling morning pages and into genuine regular creative time. I've had time to sort through years of journals and boxes of scraps of paper to find half-written poems and story ideas and put them into digital files where I can find them again. I've been able to spend quality time on putting together my poetry collection, so that in 2021 it may actually finally be done! The gift of moving forward even when everything seems static.

Of course, my 2020 gift list is much longer, full of good things that happened or that I came to appreciate, but you get the drift.

Princess Tea Zoom, Photo by Tara Collings

Moving Forward
Chris Cameron

Some runners wear headphones and listen to music or audiobooks, but I love hearing the sound of my shoes hitting the road as I run through hills of Northumberland. Different sounds for different roads: *pat-pat* on pavement; *critch-critch* on gravel; and a kind of a *wash-wash* on dirt roads.

It isn't unusual for me to run for several hours, and some people are amazed that I actually enjoy this. My reward is the peaceful contentment that comes from moving myself forward from one place to another under my own power. In the years since I moved to Meyers Island, south of Campbellford, I've run along the local roads and trails countless times, and most are as familiar to me as my own driveway.

Yet somehow, each run is slightly different, each path finds something new to throw in my way, and it is those differences that keep me guessing and engaged. Every step forward adds to my knowledge and experience for the next time.

You don't have to go out and run for hours to know that some things are hard. Home-schooling children is hard; trying to run a storefront retail business is hard; isolating yourself from loved ones is hard. They were hard during what people are calling the "before-time." They've been even harder this year. There have been more hills to climb, more trees fallen across the path.

People seem to like lamenting the loss of the good old days, and everybody is looking forward to a return to normalcy. Some on social media have been billing 2021 as some kind Elysian fields, where we can all go back to the wonderful life we led before the bad old days of 2020.

It reminds me of a Facebook group I followed for a while: a lot of people wondered why life couldn't be like it once was, when ice cream was only five cents. I suspect that if Facebook had been around back when it "once was," there would have been a group wondering why life couldn't be like it was when ice cream was only one cent.

There were no good old days, unless you count Carly Simon's maxim that they are happening today. There are just days, one after another, like steps along a path. We move forward, by running, walking, wheeling, or simply by living. We clear the hurdles any way we can and we keep going. When needed, we stop to help a fellow traveller along.

I think we should congratulate ourselves at the end of this year. It's good to see how far we've come and to collate what we've learned so we can use it on the road ahead.

I used to have a mantra I repeated in the tough parts of a very long endurance event, when the night had settled over me and all my energy was gone: *I'm alive and I'm moving forward.* As long as these two things are true, nothing else can stop us.

It's probable that 2021 will throw stuff at us we can't even imagine yet. As the late Gilda Radner reminded us, "It's always something." Who knows? Maybe someday we will look back on 2020 and sigh wistfully, remembering when *all* we had to do was wear a mask. But we will have our experience, our vision, and our humanity to help us navigate our way home.

And isn't it marvellous that we still have ice cream?

Morning Trail Run, Photo courtesy of Chris Cameron

**Morganston Tree, Photo—Ted Amsden
Photography ©2021**

Wings
Marie-Lynn Hammond

Wings. In Isabel's memory, always silver, sun-sparked. In reality, any colour; at this moment they are blue and white, like the day itself, this full blown, windblown, hot July day, all sky and snowy cumulus that swallow the earth, reducing the city to a faint smudge in the distance and rendering the airfield insignificant in comparison.

Her head thrown back, she narrows her eyes to follow the flight of the Cessna across the sun. That familiar, uncomfortable crick in the neck: we weren't designed to gaze heavenward, she thinks. So why this age-old fascination, this pull of the sky and the stars? Still, at first there's something almost comforting in the discomfort, like pulling on an old pair of boots that never quite fit. But the sense of comfort is fleeting. Before Isabel can shift her gaze from the small plane, gesture awakens memory, and the wings turn silver.

***

1964, northern Quebec. Isabel, neck craned, stands transfixed among the crowd of townsfolk who have driven to the base for Air Force Day. High overhead a fighter formation slashes the sky, sleek, menacing, their elongated nose cones half beak, half stiletto. It's almost impossible to imagine the human presence within: they look dangerous, like futuristic birds of prey. But Isabel doesn't care; she knows only that she is in thrall to their speed, their grace, their power.

That evening there is a dance at one of the messes. Isabel is persuaded to go, despite her concern for her limited English.

"*Écoute, ma belle,*" says her friend Georgette, "we are here to dance, not to discuss Shakespeare."

The fourth number is a slow dance, and a young airman walks over to Isabel.

"Hi, I'm Pete MacAllister. I'd have asked you sooner, but I'm no good at the twist."

She stammers acceptance, and he leads her out onto the floor. He's much taller than she is. Looking up she gets a general impression of blondness and a strongly cleft chin. He leads confidently. She's amazed at how light she feels, her feet barely touching the ground.

They sit together for the rest of the evening, only getting up for the slow songs. In halting English, with some frustration and much laughter, she answers his questions and asks some of her own. Yes, she lives in Chicoutimi, where she teaches grade four, but she comes from a tiny village north of Lac St-Jean. He's from Calgary, his father has done well in oil and cattle. No, no brothers or sisters—he's an only child. She chuckles and tells him she's the youngest of six girls.

He grins and puts his arm around her. "And I bet you're the prettiest of the bunch."

To cover her confusion she asks, "You are a pilot?"

"You bet. Jets, 440 Squadron, CF-104s. Starfighters, they're called."

"And you fly today, yes?"

"Sure did. Just before the Goldenhawks."

"You mean, the ones like—like birds?"

He nods.

Remembering the streamlined, predatory look of them she sighs. "Ah, they are so beautiful!"

He stares at her. "You really think so?"

She smiles. "Oh yes!"

"Now that's quite something to hear from a girl."

"*Pourquoi*? Why?"

"Because most of them say things like, 'Gee, aren't you scared flying one of those things?'" They both laugh at his imitation, and he continues, "Actually, they'll soon be phased out."

"But why?"

"Well, there's a little problem, see? They tend to fall out of the sky a lot."

He grins, cocky, so she assumes he must be joking and smiles back. Without warning, he kisses her. She looks up into his eyes, which are blue, an endless blue, like a clear sky. Suddenly she can see him in the cockpit of the fighter, slicing the air at impossible speed, those strong hands that now hold hers moving confidently at the controls. Almost faint with the sense of power that emanates from him like musk, she's falling into that infinity of blue, she's falling in love.

(Later, during their arguments about her wanting to fly, she'll remember that moment and wonder: just as she'd seen the sky reflected in his eyes, did he see, as he looked into hers, the earth? A new-ploughed, rich dark brown, a solid constant to balance his breath-taking and precarious flights?)

Within three months, they are married; within four, Isabel is pregnant. Because they live on the Bagotville base, in the box-like, government-issue housing known as PMQs—Permanent Married Quarters—flying becomes a vicarious part of her life. That first fall when Pete's away on training, she puts on her warmest clothes some nights and steals down to the hangars, getting as close as possible without being noticed. Hidden in shadow she watches, junkie seeking a fix; listening to the cryptic shouts of the ground crew and breathing in the sweet, cloudy fumes of gasoline, she waits for the moment when the engines finally rev up. Pulse beating faster now as the fighters roar past, gathering speed like darkness around them, gathering her in too, till at last the night sky snatches them up and they vanish, leaving only thunder to ring in her ears, leaving her grounded while the northern lights dance mockingly above.

The baby is born in June. A girl, Sylvie. ("Better luck next time," jokes a buddy of Pete's when he thinks Isabel is out of earshot. "Hey, this is just a warm-up!" Pete jokes back.) The baby's eyes, dark like Isabel's at birth, begin to change soon after and promise to be as blue as her father's. At first Isabel is completely absorbed in this new world of mothering, but by the time Sylvie is three, she's starting to feel restless. Pete suggests she go back to teaching; the hitch is that they've received a posting and in two months will be in Cold Lake, Alberta, where Isabel's poor English and her Quebec certificate will bar her from work.

One night she finally tells him: "Pete, I want to learn to fly."

At first he's incredulous, then becomes almost pouty, like a ten-year-old boy who finds out the girls have discovered the secret fort and want in.

"Jesus, Isabel! Why the hell would you want to do that?"

"For the same reasons you do it," she replies, evenly. He remains silent, his back to her. Now she tries to placate. "Pete, of course I do not mean to fly jets! But why not a small plane? It's not so strange! I read stories about women who fly them!"

"Yes, but it's—it's *dangerous*!" he explodes, as if hoping to frighten her back to her senses.

She chooses to let him think he's won, but in the next few weeks she locates a small flying school near Arvida. Knowing it's impractical to begin lessons before they move, she contents herself with buying a basic navigational text, which she hides. The nights that Pete is flying she lies awake, listening for the distant rumble of engines and imagining herself soaring skyward over forest and rock pitted with indigo lakes. One night she realizes, with a small shock of surprise, that in these fantasies her husband is not there. She is always flying alone.

***

The night of the accident it was raining, a bitter early spring rain, and Isabel had just put Sylvie to bed when Pete came into the living room with her flying text in hand.

"For godsake, Isabel," he said, "this is crazy! You should be getting pregnant, not wasting your time on this!"

From there the argument escalated, taking in all the petty and not-so-petty grievances they'd managed to stock-pile in their three years of marriage. They were well into the battle, Pete pacing and shouting, Isabel shouting back, when the phone rang. It was the squadron, they wanted Pete: a kind of surprise scramble. There had been several lately, in response to the sudden increase of Russian fighters testing NORAD's coastal defences.

"Damn it!" he said, grabbing his flying suit. "We'll continue this tonight." And he was gone.

Later, after the investigation was unable to identify a definitive reason for the crash—"Cause obscure," read the final statement—Isabel replayed those last moments over and over again. Where had she first heard that a good Air Force wife never fights with her husband on the nights he must fly? But I didn't *know* they were going to call him, she kept telling herself. Anyway, who says it was her fault? Lack of clear evidence of mechanical failure didn't rule out such a failure. ("There's a little problem, see? They tend to fall out of the sky a lot.")

The plane went down, she discovered to her horror, less than two miles from her home village. Wreckage had been strewn throughout the forest, forest she might well have hiked in as a teenager. As for Pete's body, she didn't ask; she didn't want to know. His family arranged the funeral. When the coffin was carried into the church, Isabel fainted and her mother took her home.

Since then, whenever Isabel closes her eyes, she sees an image of a forest clearing, littered with twisted metal, still and silent and glinting faintly in the weak sunlight of spring. At night the image becomes a nightmare. Pete stumbles out of the woods, covered in blood, groping towards Isabel, who recoils in horror and then wakes up, heart pounding. She eventually moves south to Hull, where the landscape is softer, less likely to conjure memories. For a while she's terrified at the thought of flying. In time, the horror recedes, the fears fade. The tear-stained photographs are put away, except for one on Sylvie's dresser: a shot of Pete in the cockpit of the CF-104, looking like a young god but grinning like the devil.

Isabel marries again, a father for Sylvie, a solid, quiet man. There's little passion between them, but no arguments either. Sylvie loves him, but as she gets older she becomes more and more fascinated with the mythical hero in the photographs. And as Isabel speaks of Pete, her old dream of flying begins to stir. Apprehension stirs too, but she tells herself this may be the way to lay her ghosts to rest.

She enrols for flying lessons. With the instructor beside her in the cockpit she is all eagerness and humorous self-deprecation, while privately battling small waves of terror. "You're doing just fine," he tells her. "Not long till you won't need me."

The morning of her solo flight she feels quite confident. Her husband and Sylvie, now a gawky thirteen, have come to cheer her on. But something happens as she taxis down the runway. Her fingers turn to ice, a film forms over her eyes, she's in the clearing surrounded by wreckage and metal shards; green light filters through the branches like a poisonous gas. She can't breathe. Dimly she senses that not only fear, but guilt, is still lurking. She gropes for the throttle and pulls back hard. She can't leave the ground. She's trapped.

Two years later she tries once more; once more she freezes just before take-off. She doesn't try again. Sometimes though, she dreams she's piloting a small plane, as light and fragile as a glider. Then the dream shifts and the plane disappears, yet she's still flying. She panics and immediately starts to fall, then realizes she is actually in control. Exhilarated, she arcs upward again, riding the currents of warm blue air. When she looks at her outstretched arms, she sees they've turned to wings.

***

The blue-and-white Cessna banks into a turn and begins its downward journey. Anxiously Isabel watches, assessing the angle of descent. Too fast, she thinks. *Mon dieu*—pull back now! she silently orders the pilot, who appears to agree and is circling again. This time the little plane touches down smoothly and comes to a stop at the end of the runway.

The young pilot climbs out. For a moment Isabel's heart catches. It's Pete she's seeing, the fair hair and lanky build, the stubborn, cocky set of the jaw. But above all, the casual confidence and grace.

As the instructor, a big burly man, strides over, the pilot calls out, "*J'ai reussi, Maman*—I flew solo!" Sylvie is grinning. "Was I okay or what!"

Isabel swallows hard and rushes to embrace her daughter. "*T'étais merveilleuse!*" she exclaims.

"Well done," says the instructor. "Congrats!"

"I, uh, came in a little steep there the first time." Sylvie sounds a bit sheepish.

"I noticed that," the instructor says, and they all laugh.

Sylvie stops laughing. Her eyes search her mother's face, and she says, "I think he'd be sort of proud of me, don't you?"

Isabel remembers the fights twenty years ago and wonders for a moment. But a daughter is not a wife, she thinks. Children—even daughters, when there are no sons—are encouraged to follow in their father's footsteps. Anyway, the world has changed. If Pete had lived, surely by now he'd be a different person? Surely he might even understand Isabel's desire too? Yes, she decides. Of course he would. I was not wrong to want it.

"He would be so proud," Isabel says. "*Comme moi.*"

Sylvie glows, and for a moment, Isabel sees Pete smiling back in those clear blue eyes.

Suddenly something is released in her. The last fragment of guilt, sharp as a jagged piece of steel, softens and works loose. She feels it lifting away, becoming smaller and smaller until it finally vanishes.

Railway Line at Sunset, Ted Amsden Photography
©2021

Contributors to this book:

Ted Amsden was the Poet Laureate of Cobourg for six years because he could shout in public. He recently completed, *The Last of The Red Hot Egos,* a novel about a photojournalist working in a declining newsroom on a story about closemouthed cops who finds when his past comes calling he suddenly has a story for the ages.

Kim Aubrey's stories, essays, and poems have appeared in journals and anthologies, including *Best Canadian Stories, Event,* **Numero Cinq, Room** and **The New Quarterly.**
Her story collection, **What We Hold in Our Hands,** won an Honorable Mention in the Bermuda Literary Awards.

Christopher Black has had a varied career as lawyer, actor, and writer but now spends most of his time writing, or playing classical guitar. His novel *Beneath The Clouds* has received positive reviews and his recent collection of poetry, *Poems From A Passing Stranger,* awaits them. His blog, called *One Voyce of the World,* can be found at: **https://christopher-black.com**

Alan F. Bland is a saxophonist, photographer, kayaker, cook and writer who has had several of his short stories published while hoping to unleash some of his longer fiction on an unsuspecting public. Meantime he writes legal opinions as an expert witness for trials at the Ontario Superior Courts of Justice.

Mia Burrus explores the boundaries and spaces between urban and wild, spoken and silent, fleeting and timeless, free-formed and structured, known and unknowable, mindless and mindful, through poetry, photography and bricolage **www.miaburrus.com**

Patricia Calder is currently inspired by her grandmother's scrapbook of World War II. Through letters, telegrams, pictures, and news clippings written by her uncle, Jack Calder RCAF navigator, his story is revealed. From the pieces of this puzzle, she is reconstructing his life from 1940-1944 in a historical fiction. https://patriciacalder.ca/

Christopher Cameron, a veteran writer and editor, combines his passion for the arts with his respect for the power and beauty of the written word. He is the editor of *Watershed* Magazine and the author of *Dr. Bartolo's Umbrella*, a memoir of his three decades as an opera singer. www.lyricycle.ca

Michael Croucher is an award-winning writer of novels and short stories. He writes crime and general fiction, as well as personal narratives. He lives in Cobourg, Ontario, with his wife of 53 years. They have two daughters and five grandchildren. Facebook Link — www.facebook.com/mikecroucher.754

Ann Di Nardo is a photographer who works almost exclusively with an iPhone. Colour and light are her primary subjects.

Antony Di Nardo is the author of five books of poetry, most recently, *SKYLIGHT* and *GONE MISSNG*. His poem "May June July" was winner of Exile's Poetry Prize and nominated for a National Magazine Award. His work has been translated into several languages and can be found in journals across Canada and internationally.

Marie-Lynn Hammond is a bilingual singer-songwriter, playwright, writer, editor, and occasional poet who moved to Cobourg six years ago. A founding member of Stringband, one of Canada's seminal folk groups, she's known for her original songs, which range from hilarious to haunting and often tell uniquely Canadian stories. http://marielynnhammond.com/ http://marielynnhammond.com/writer/true-stories/the-dress-a-memoir/

Carolyn Muir Helfenstein is author of *Why Not?* a memoir of running a small weekly newspaper—and later, *Rock Solid*, a three-generational saga that helped Carolyn regain an original, Newfoundland identity. Recently her writing includes *Family Love* (Robert Fear ed. Britain) and *My fate*—Impact Stories—University of Waterloo. Facebook Page: Carolyn-Muir-Helfenstein https://uwaterloo.ca/impact-stories/my-fate https://www.fd81.net/freds-blog/family-love-by-carolyn-muir-helfenstein

Katie Hoogendam is a writer, interdisciplinary artist and educator who lives and works in Northumberland County. Her poems, essays and other writing have been published across Canada and the US. Her current creative project can be found here: https://www.patreon.com/we3

Linda Hutsell-Manning, born in Winnipeg, attended Ryerson, teachers' college and Guelph University. She's published 13 children's books, a novella, *Heads I Win,* a novel, *That Summer in Franklin* (Second Story Press), a two-act comedy, *A Certain Singing Teacher* and her memoir, *Fearless and Determined,* Blue Denim Press 2019. www.lindahutsellmanning.ca_ https://www.youtube.com/watch?v=x6C-5IKx-L4&feature=youtu.be

Shane Joseph is a Canadian novelist, blogger, reviewer, short story writer and publisher. He is the author of six novels and three collections of short stories. His latest novel, *Circles in the Spiral,* was released in October 2020. For details visit his website at http://www.shanejoseph.com/ www.https://www.facebook.com/shane.joseph.

Peggy Dymond Leavey is the author of nine novels for young readers, with three nominated for the Silver Birch Award. As well as books and articles, Peggy has published three biographies of Canadian

women. A member of several arts associations and The Writers Union of Canada, Peggy lives in Quinte West.
http://peggydymondleavey.com
facebook.com/peggy.dymond.leavey.author

Kathryn MacDonald's poetry has been published in literary journals in Canada, the U.S., England, and Ireland. Her poem "Duty / *Deon*" won *Arc Poetry Magazine*'s Award of Awesomeness (February, 2021) and "Seduction" was short-listed for the 2019 Freefall Poetry Contest. She is the author of *A Breeze You Whisper* (poems, 2011) and *Calla & Édourd* (fiction, 2009). Website: https://KathrynMacDonald.com.

Ronald Mackay, in addition to engaging in development projects designed to enhance food security in many countries, has taught at universities in Europe, Asia and the Americas. He has published three memoirs in English, one in Spanish and many short stories in anthologies. He also writes plays for community theatre.
https://www.amazon.com/~/e/B001JXCBL8

Maureen Mullally is an artist and writer, who has lived in Northumberland County for more than 30 years. She has written and illustrated stories for all four of the *Hill Spirits* anthologies and has recently self-published a memoir of her life before, during and after WW2.

Reva Nelson has found that her move to Cobourg has brought new friends and greater creativity. The author *of Risk It!, Bounce Back!* and *Hippie Chick Abroad* has now published a book of poetry, *Twisted Branches*. She can be contacted at revanelson77@gmail.com or www.revanelson.ca

Jessica Outram is Poet Laureate of Cobourg, a principal, playwright, podcast host, and creativity coach. She loves singing Eva Cassidy songs, taking pictures in nature, learning to garden, and using

intuition to paint. She is a proud citizen of the Métis Nation of Ontario who continually enriches her life through the teachings of her ancestors. Learn more at
www.sunshineinajar.com or www.creativitycoaching.ca

Tom Pickering's writing career started in technical documentation. Then he discovered community theatre. Starting out as an actor, he switched to writing and directing his original plays. *Skates Off* is one in a series of short stories featuring the early life experiences of a boy named Will.

Marie Prins' mid-grade novel, *The Girl From the Attic*, was the Common Deer Press 2019 Uncommon Quest Silver Winner and was released in October, 2020. Her writing, including memoir and poetry, is inspired by the history of her home and its gardens.
https://marieprins.ca/the-girl-from-the-attic/
https://marieprins.ca/wp-content/uploads/TGFTA-video.mp4
https://www.kirkusreviews.com/book-reviews/marie-prins/the-girl-from-the-attic/

Felicity Sidnell Reid is a poet, short story and memoir writer whose work has been published in a variety of anthologies and journals. Her novel *Alone: Winter in the Woods* (Hidden Brook Press) has recently been released as an e-book. She is the co-host of the radio series,
Word on the Hills.
Website: http://felicitysidnellreid.com/

Cynthia Reyes' work as an author follows an award-winning career in television. Her books include the *Myrtle the Purple Turtle* series for children, and, for adults, *A Good Home, An Honest House* and *Twigs in My Hair*. Her writing has also been published in anthologies, newspapers, magazines, and on her blog, cynthiasreyes.com.
https://www.amazon.ca/kindle-dbs/entity/author/B00F1HTQQ6

Erika Rummel taught history at University of Toronto and Wilfrid Laurier. The author of over a dozen books of social history and six novels, she won a lifetime achievement award from the Renaissance Society of America (2018). *The Inquisitor's Niece*, won best historical novel of the year from the Colorado Publishers' Association. www.erikarummel.com. http://rummelsincrediblestories.blogspot.com/.

Gwynn Scheltema has been a columnist, freelancer and a fiction editor for *Lichen Arts & Letters Preview*. Her award-winning fiction and poetry have appeared in literary magazines and anthologies. She co-hosts *Word on the Hills* radio show on Northumberland 89.7FM, and writes, edits, coaches and teaches creative writing through www.writescape.ca.

René Schmidt is a member of S.O.H., the Writer's Union of Canada and Author's Booking Service. His novel, *Leaving Fletchville*, was the Red Maple Honour Book winner in 2010. His *Canadian Disasters* books have collectively sold more than 100,000 copies. He is not planning on writing about the pandemic. Yet. Visit his web page at reneschmidt.ca

Allan Seymour is relatively new to writing, having completed three unpublished stories. His favourite genre is historical fiction. Al loves researching historical characters. Prior to retiring to Cobourg, Al ran his own contracting company, was a logistics consultant and manufacturing manager. He also co-founded three charitable organizations

Janet Stobie is a writer, storyteller, and ordained minister. She has written two novels, 3 short story collections, 3 children's books and a worship resource. She writes a blog and column in a local paper. A resident of Peterborough, Janet spends her retirement writing, enjoying family, and having fun. Buy her books at https://janetstobie.com/

https://www.youtube.com/watch?v=BMx6jRU8Uqc
https://www.youtube.com/watch?v=wi8jvgzkGrI

Diane Taylor has written two books, one about writing a memoir, and one about living aboard a sailboat. She lived for three years in the Turks and Caicos Islands where she grew algae to feed baby conch. She gives a course on memoir writing to encourage people to leave behind memories and love for future generations.
Website: www.dianemtaylor.com

Donna Wootton is a graduate of the Humber School for Writers. Her nonfiction book about her Dad, *Moon Remembered,* was published by Ginger Press. Her novel, *What Shirley Missed,* was published by Hidden Brook Press. Her poetry on Cuba was published in the anthology *The Divinity of Blue.*
www.dmwootton.com

Eric E. Wright served in Pakistan as a missionary teacher for 16 years, after which he pastored churches in Ontario. Twelve of his books have been published including 4 novels and a memoir. He and his wife Mary Helen have 3 children and 9 grandchildren.
Web site: http://www.countrywindow.ca Facebook: Eric E Wright
Blog: https://ericewright.wordpress.com/